# THE COLD WAR IN VAL-D'OR

A History of the Ukrainian Community
of Val-d'Or, Quebec

MYRON MOMRYK

(January 1, 2020)

# THE COLD WAR IN VAL-D'OR

A History of the Ukrainian Community of Val-d'Or, Quebec

MYRON MOMRYK

(January 1, 2020)

Library and Archives Canada Cataloguing in Publication

Title: The Cold War in Val-d'Or: a history of the Ukrainian community in Val-d'Or, Quebec / Myron Momryk.
Names: Momryk, Myron, 1946- author.

Identifiers: Canadiana (print) 20200298593 | Canadiana (ebook) 20200298771 | ISBN 9781771615167 (softcover) | ISBN 9781771615174 (PDF) | ISBN 9781771615181 (EPUB) | ISBN 9781771615198 (Kindle)

Subjects: LCSH: Ukrainians—Québec (Province)—Val-d'Or—History—20th century. | LCSH: Ukrainians—Québec (Province)—Val-d'Or—Social conditions—20th century. | LCSH: Ukrainians—Québec (Province)—Val-d'Or—Social life and customs—20th century. | LCSH: Val-d'Or (Québec)—History—20th century. | LCSH: Val-d'Or (Québec)—Social conditions—20th century. | LCSH: Val-d'Or (Québec)—Social life and customs—20th century.

Classification: LCC FC2949.V35 Z76 2020 | DDC 971.4/13900491791009045—dc23

No part of this book may be reproduced or transmitted in any form, by any means, electronic or mechanical, including photocopying and recording, information storage and retrieval systems, without permission in writing from the publisher, except by a reviewer who may quote a brief passage in a review.

Published by Mosaic Press, Oakville, Ontario, Canada, 2020.

MOSAIC PRESS, Publishers
Copyright © Myron Momryk, 2020

Designed by Andrea Tempesta
andreatempesta@yahoo.com • www.flickr.com/photos/andreatempesta

Cover photo: VE Day in Val-d'Or, 8 May, 1945 with Soviet and pro-Tito Yugoslav flags. Photo credit: La Société d'histoire et de généalogie de Val-d'Or.

We acknowledge the Ontario Arts Council for their support of our publishing program

**MOSAIC PRESS** 1252 Speers Road, Units 1 & 2, Oakville, Ontario, L6L 5N9
(905) 825-2130 • info@mosaic-press.com • www.mosaic-press.com

Dedicated to the memory of my parents,
Steve Momryk (1918-2005) and Katherine Wowk (1923-2001)

## ABBREVIATIONS

| | | | |
|---|---|---|---|
| **AO** | Archives of Ontario | **RCMP** | Royal Canadian Mounted Police |
| **AUUC** | Association of United Ukrainian Canadians *(Tovarystvo obiednanykh ukrainskykh kanadtsiv)* | **SUM** | Ukrainian Youth Organization *(Spilka ukrainskoi molodi or CYM)* |
| | | **UCA** | Ukrainian Canadian Association |
| **CIUS** | Canadian Institute of Ukrainian Studies | **UNYF** | Ukrainian National Youth Federation of Canada *(Molod ukrainskoho natsionalnoho obiednannia or MUNO)* |
| **CPC** | Communist Party of Canada | | |
| **CSIS** | Canadian Security and Intelligence Service | **UNF** | Ukrainian National Federation of Canada *(Ukrainske natsionalne obiednannia or UNO)* |
| **DP** | Displaced Persons | | |
| **FRC** | Federation of Russian Canadians | | |
| **LAC** | Library and Archives Canada | **ULFTA** | Ukrainian Labour - Farmer Temple Association *(Tovarystvo ukrainskyi robitnycho - farmerskyi dim or TURFDim)* |
| **LPP** | Labour Progressive Party *(also Communist Party of Canada)* | | |
| **NAC** | National Archives of Canada | | |
| **OUK** | Ukrainian Women's Organization of Canada *(Orhanizatsiia ukrainok Kanady)* | **USDP** | Ukrainian Social Democratic Party |
| | | **WBA** | Workers Benevolent Association of Canada *(Robitnyche zapomohove tovarystvo)* |
| **PQ** | Parti Québécois | | |
| **RCAF** | Royal Canadian Air Force | **YCL** | Young Communist League |

TABLE OF CONTENTS

| | |
|---|---|
| Preface | 9 |
| Introduction | 11 |
| Acknowledgements | 17 |
| | |
| Outline of Ukrainian Immigration to Canada | 18 |
| Abitibi | 21 |
| The Spirit Lake Internment Camp – 1915-1916 | 23 |
| The Sheptetski Colony – 1928-1935 | 27 |
| The Abitibi Gold Rush – 1923-1939 | 30 |
| The Second Wave of Ukrainian Immigration – 1924-1939 | 34 |
| The Early Years – 1933-1939 | 37 |
| The Second World War – 1939-1945 | 49 |
| The Displaced Persons: The Third Wave of Ukrainian Immigration – 1946-1952 | 66 |
| Building the Community – 1950-1954 | 83 |
| The School Question – 1948-1956 | 92 |
| Building the Ukrainian Catholic Church – 1953-1954 | 95 |
| Continuity and Change – 1954-1967 | 97 |
| The Decline of the Community – 1967-1991 | 117 |
| The Legacy | 125 |
| Conclusion | 131 |
| | |
| Appendix | 138 |
| Maps | 140 |
| Endnotes | 142 |
| Bibliography | 171 |

# PREFACE

As a specialist in the history of Ukrainians in Canada, I am very pleased that this study by Myron Momryk is devoted to a Ukrainian community in a part of the country that is often overlooked or simply overshadowed by the attention that gets paid to rural settlements on the prairies or in large urban centers. Quebec Ukrainians, in particular, tend to be under-researched, notwithstanding some useful work that has been done over the years on aspects of Ukrainian organizational life in the province.

The case of Val-d'Or is especially interesting, being a city situated 530 kilometers northwest of Montreal and in many respects similar to the mining communities with significant Ukrainian populations established around the same time in Kirkland Lake and Timmins, across the border in Ontario. These and other cities and towns that grew around resource industries in remote areas of the Canadian Shield have a distinct make-up, which was naturally reflected in their Ukrainian organizational activity. Having a strong working-class character, they frequently witnessed strikes and labour unrest that were influenced in no small part by ideological differences between radical trade unionists sympathetic to the Communist Party and the Soviet Union, and the often more conservative immigrants from Ukraine. Although seemingly far removed from world events, the Cold War was very much a factor in some of the developments that took place in the one-industry settlements in the northern reaches of Ontario and Quebec. The great value of Mr. Momryk's study is that it documents how these issues played out among Ukrainians while telling the story of a Ukrainian community that almost nothing has been written about.

Jars Balan
Director
Canadian Institute of Ukrainian Studies
University of Alberta
Edmonton, Alberta

# INTRODUCTION

The research and writing of this local history of the Ukrainian community in Val-d'Or began as a series of small projects and presentations while working at the Library and Archives Canada (LAC) in Ottawa in the years after 1981. During my research on Ukrainian Canadian historical topics, I was able to identify historical information in federal government records and in several private archival fonds on Ukrainian individuals and organizations across Canada including Val-d'Or. I became interested in the local history of the Ukrainian community in Val-d'Or in an attempt to better explain the events and evolution of the community because of its unique situation as a one-industry town in a French Canadian milieu. Further information was located in other archival institutions in Toronto and elsewhere. Relevant publications, newspaper articles and academic dissertations were consulted in the LAC, Archives of Ontario, University of Ottawa Library and material obtained through the inter-library loan system. I lived in Val-d'Or with my parents from 1949 until 1965 and I was witness to many of the events described in this story.

An early draft of this study was prepared for the Canadian Ethnic Studies Association Conference held in Montreal in 1985. With the approach of the Centennial of the first two Ukrainian immigrants to Canada in 1991, a further effort was made to research the local history. A summary of this study, The Ukrainian Community in Val d'Or-Bourlamaque, Quebec, was published by the Ukrainian Canadian Centennial Commission of Montreal in the publication edited by Alexander Biega and Myroslav Diakowsky, *The Ukrainian Experience in Quebec, The Basilian Press, Toronto* (1994). This present study is a revised, updated and enlarged version of the earlier article.

Shortly after the publication of this book in 1994, I was able to obtain information that the Canadian Security and Intelligence Service (CSIS) held a file of approximately 1,100 pages relating to the Val-d'Or Branch of the Association of United Ukrainian Canadians (AUUC). This document was compiled by the Security Service of the Royal Canadian Mounted Police (RCMP) and inherited by CSIS after the creation of this agency in 1984. This document is preserved in the Library and Archives Canada. I applied under the Access to Information Act to examine this material and this new source of rare historical information encouraged me to continue my research and writing. In June, 2003, I submitted another request for access to files relating to the activities of the local branches of the Canadian Slav Committee and also the Federation of Russian Canadians. Copies of these documents were made available in June, 2004. This large file encouraged me to re-write the history of the Ukrainian community in Val-d'Or as a Cold War story. Since much of the information is based on the RCMP file and the RCMP was critical of the Ukrainian left-wing movement, this attitude and interpretation can be found in almost all the RCMP reports cited in this story.[1]

A copy of the Ukrainian Catholic Church parish register was deposited by Rev. Leo Chayka with the Val-d'Or Historical Society and it provided information on births, marriages and deaths in the parish. The records of the Val-d'Or Roman Catholic Cemetery were also examined for further information. Both the Roman Catholic and Protestant Cemeteries were visited on several occasions over the years to study the biographical information on the monuments. Additional material regarding the early Ukrainian prospectors was located and included in the text.

This study is limited to the Ukrainian community in Val-d'Or and region, that is, Val-d'Or and Bourlamaque with passing references to Perron[2] and Malartic. Information on the Ukrainian settlement at Sheptetski (Sheptytsky, Lac Castagnier) and the Spirit Lake Internment Camp near Amos, Quebec, is included to describe the early years of the Ukrainian presence in Abitibi. In other words, this study includes those locations that were within the responsibility of the Ukrainian Catholic parish of Val-d'Or. It does not include the Ukrainian community in Rouyn-Noranda that deserves its own study.

The official names of the Ukrainian churches in Canada were and continues to be the Greek Catholic and Greek Orthodox Churches (that

INTRODUCTION

is, according to the Byzantine Greek rather than the Roman rite). But in Canada, a tradition developed to designate them as the Ukrainian Catholic and Ukrainian Orthodox Churches that in some cases, confused the census-takers and various government officials. Both designations are used in this story.

Throughout this study there are constant references to the 'Ukrainian' community in Val-d'Or. It should be clarified, however, that the correct designation is always 'Ukrainian Canadian'. Although, certain individuals and organizations described themselves as 'Ukrainian' and were perceived by others, especially other East European groups, as 'Ukrainian', this designation was and continues to be a normal part of living in Val-d'Or and in Canada.

In Val-d'Or, the French Canadians always made a distinction between their community and the 'others'.[3] Ukrainians were placed in the category of the 'others' and were often described as part of the local Anglophone community. However, it should be remembered that as 'Ukrainians', they were and are as distinct from Ukrainians in Ukraine as from other Canadians. It would be a serious historical error to equate the Ukrainians from Val-d'Or, especially those born and educated there, as somehow identical to the present-day citizens of Ukraine. Over the decades, the Ukrainian community in Val-d'Or became an exclusively Canadian community. However, due to the present-day Canadian tradition of identifying specific ethnocultural communities according to their ancestral origins, individuals and organizations will continue to be recognized and described as 'Ukrainian' rather than as 'Ukrainian Canadian' in this study. The term 'French Canadian' is used throughout this study although the more modern designation is 'Québécois'.

One of the main difficulties in researching this study was obtaining access to historical information on the left-wing Ukrainian community in Val-d'Or other than the RCMP records. The main sources of information were the Ukrainian left-wing newspapers, *Narodna Hazeta (The People's Gazette)* and later, *Zhyttia i Slovo (Life and Word)*. Although some individuals in Val-d'Or were no doubt members of the Communist Party of Canada (CPC), this was not the case with everyone whose

13

name appears in this study as a member of the Ukrainian pro-left organizations and their community. Members had their own reasons for belonging to this political segment of the community that supported the Soviet Union and Soviet Ukraine and opposed to the local pro-nationalist Ukrainians. Some individuals supported the left-wing community through personal friendships and common difficult experiences especially during the Depression of the 1930s. Others were barely literate in English and Ukrainian and accepted the vision and interpretation of the world as offered by the Communist Party members. In this study, they are described as pro-left or pro-communist or even communist, but it should be remembered that exceptions could always be made in individual cases. In the later years, several individuals became inactive members of the pro-left community while others drifted away. Upon their deaths, a few funerals were held according to the rites of one of the local Protestant churches and there were rare individuals whose funerals were held in the Ukrainian Catholic or Russian Orthodox Churches. It is evident from the information in the RCMP files that one or more members of the left-wing community in Val-d'Or were informants for the RCMP. Their identities remain unknown. However, members of the pro-nationalist Ukrainian community perceived the active members of the pro-communist community as opponents of the Ukrainian nationalist movement throughout their lives. This was another fundamental division among the members of the Ukrainian community in Val-d'Or.

When names of Ukrainian residents of Val d'Or are mentioned in Ukrainian-language publications, they are transliterated according to a modified Library of Congress system. If names are printed in English and French-language publications, the names are included in the text as spelled including, in some cases, several variations of the spelling.

Traditionally, the spelling of the name of the town was 'Val D'Or' but after the amalgamation with Boulamaque, the official name became 'Val-d'Or'. Where the traditional spelling appears in publications, documents, newspapers, it is retained in this publication. In the years after amalgamation, the name is spelled in the book according to the contemporary style.

## INTRODUCTION

The French-speaking population of Quebec is described as 'French Canadian' in this story and as 'Québécois' after the 1960s with the evolution of politics and national identity in Quebec.

A basic purpose of this 'micro-history' is to create a record of the Ukrainian community in Val-d'Or that has for all practical purposes disappeared. Also, this story hopefully will encourage further studies of Ukrainian communities in eastern Canada especially in the years after the Second World War. Of particular interest is the influence of the Ukrainian Displaced Persons who formed the third wave of Ukrainian immigration to Canada (1945-1952). Former residents of Val-d'Or are encouraged to write autobiographies, biographies, memoirs and family histories that could be valuable sources for further historical study. It is hoped that with a large selection of local history studies, it will be possible to arrive at some general and also, more critical conclusions concerning the evolution of the Ukrainian Canadian community at the national level and also the larger Canadian community.

## ACKNOWLEDGEMENTS

During the research and writing of this story, I have benefitted from conversations and interviews with a number of individuals who had some connection or knowledge of the ethnocultural communities in Val-d'Or-Bourlamaque. I would like to thank these individuals for their contributions. Any errors in facts and interpretation are entirely my own.

Nick Andrusyshyn
Denys Chabot
Harry Diaczyk
Al Hnatiuk
Donna Kalynchuk (1945-2018)
Miroslaw (Rick) Kaminski (1947-2019)
Stanley Klosevych (1927-2015)
Dr. Edward Laine (1940-2003)
Ivan (John) Lenyk (Died 1993)
Mike Sikorsky (1947-2017)
Robert (Ihor) Sikorsky
Sally Smoly
Odette Vincent-Domey (1948-2002)

I would also like to thank Christine Habrowych, Keith Male and especially Olena Lytwyn for their assistance with the preparation of an earlier version of this manuscript for publication. Thanks are also due to Howard Aster and Andrea Tempesta for their contributions to the publication of this book.

The two maps were prepared by Lev Piaseckyj.

Publication of this book has been made possible through a grant from The Taras Shevchenko Foundation, Ukrainian Canadian Veterans' Fund.

## OUTLINE OF UKRAINIAN IMMIGRATION TO CANADA

In 1891, the first two Ukrainian settlers arrived in Canada. They were followed in the years 1892-1914 by approximately 170,000 immigrants from Halychyna (Galicia) in the Austro-Hungarian Empire[4] forming the first wave of Ukrainian immigration to Canada. Prior to 1891, there were individuals from what is now Ukraine traveling, visiting and in some cases living in Canada and they were of German, Russian, Jewish and Mennonite origin including some migrants with Ukrainian-sounding names. This first and largest wave of Ukrainian immigration to Canada arrived in search of new land for farming since there was a growing land shortage and general poverty in Halychyna. The Ukrainian pioneers were met by the Anglo-Canadian and French Canadian host societies and a federal government intent on settling the frontiers of Canada.[5] The first (1892-1914) and also the second waves (1920-1939) of Ukrainian settlers were directed primarily to the agricultural frontier in western Canada. Prior to 1921, these immigrants were identified in federal government records as Ruthenians, Galicians, Bukovynians and even as Poles, Russians and Austrians. They brought with them memories of the social and political conditions in Austria-Hungary that restricted Ukrainian political, social and economic development. In some cases, they also brought political ideas that supported a more radical and even a revolutionary approach to politics and contemporary problems. They also brought memories of village life based on the Greek Catholic and Greek Orthodox Churches and community organizations that shaped their Ukrainian culture and identity. The first Ukrainian immigrants were almost entirely from the peasant population of Halychyna (Galicia) and Bukovyna (Bukovina) in the Austro-Hungarian Empire, now in western Ukraine. About ten percent of the immigrants came from the central Ukrainian lands in the Imperial Russian Empire. They became known in the popular press and literature at that time as 'the men in sheepskin coats'. The Depression of the 1930s and the successive crop failures on farms in the prairies obliged many settlers to seek employment across Canada including the mining frontiers in northern Ontario and Quebec. In a few cases, some returned to Halychyna then part of eastern Poland where they still had family and owned land. The third wave of Ukrainian immigration (1947-1952) was directed mainly to the lumber, mining and industrial frontiers in eastern Canada. The post-Second World War immigration was largely from what is now western Ukraine but included Ukrainians from Soviet Ukraine and represented a wider spectrum of occupations and regions. They brought with them their political 'baggage' based on their experiences of surviving during and after the Second World War. This 'baggage' formed the basis of their political convictions and attitudes for the remainder of their lives in Canada.

As a result of political developments in Poland during the 1980s, a number of young Ukrainians were able to leave Poland and seek sanctuary in Canada. These were mainly descendants of those Ukrainians who were resettled after the Second World War from the eastern border and Lemko areas to northern and western Poland. Most of these young Ukrainians settled in the larger urban centres in Canada; they formed their own associations or joined existing organizations and contributed to the Ukrainian community. A fourth wave of Ukrainian immigration began after the declaration of Ukrainian independence on August 24, 1991. Again, many of these immigrants were young, educated and in many cases, already spoke English or French. They were able to integrate into the existing Ukrainian and larger Canadian community without many of the obstacles encountered by earlier waves of immigration.

During the 1920s and 1930s, a significant percentage of the new Ukrainian immigrants sought employment in small resource-based communities in the frontier areas of eastern and northern Canada. Their history was shaped to a large extent by the socio-economic structure of these one-industry towns[6] as well as by the broader historical forces that shaped Ukrainian Canadian and Canadian society as a whole. After the Second World War, these towns received the Ukrainian and other Displaced Persons (DPs) who brought additional numbers and new energy that perpetuated community life for several more decades. The history of the Ukrainian community in Val-d'Or-Bourlamaque is typical of many similar ethnocultural communities in one-industry towns across Canada. And this history is also an important part of Ukrainian Canadian and Canadian history.

# ABITIBI

Val-d'Or is located in the Abitibi region of Quebec, approximately 420 kilometers north-west of Montreal and about 340 kilometers north-north-west of Ottawa. The town lies along the height of the Canadian Shield and in the eastern part of the geological formation known as the Cadillac-Bouzan Fault.[7] Rivers in the area flow north into James Bay and only a few kilometers away, other rivers begin to flow south into the Ottawa River system. The area, covered by rivers flowing into James Bay and Hudson Bay, formed part of the territory assigned to the Hudson Bay Company. By 1898, the Témiscamingue and Abitibi region was part of the province of Quebec. From the earliest years, this region was known mainly as a source of furs to the Hudson Bay Company. In the 1880s and 1890s, the area was explored by geologists from the Canadian Geological Service and by French Canadian clergy intent on converting the local aboriginal peoples and occupying the land for the French Canadians. During this period, rivers and lakes were given the names of prominent Canadians and also names of missionary clergy mostly members of the Oblate Order replacing the original aboriginal names. The completion of the National Transcontinental Railway in 1912 opened the Abitibi region to further prospecting and agricultural settlement.

The large Clay Belt that extends across Northeastern Ontario and Northwestern Quebec provided some areas of potential farmland. However, the swamp, muskeg, rocks, bush and large numbers of lakes and rivers along with the long winters and short summers made farming a risky gamble at best. Farmers were also challenged in the summers by forest fires, migrating animals, clouds of mosquitoes, black flies and other insects. The long distances to markets and the tendency for frost to appear even in June and snow in September discouraged all but the most dedicated farmers.

The Abitibi region was always distinguished by its remoteness. Although there have been significant improvements to road, rail, bus and air travel and also media and electronic communications between Abitibi and the rest of Quebec, this region is still considered as 'isolated' from the large centres such as Montreal and Quebec City. Among some specialist occupations, Val-d'Or is viewed by some young university graduates from Montreal as a 'hardship' post. The geography of the region had a fundamental influence on the character and development of the various farming and mining communities including the Ukrainian community in Val-d'Or and Bourlamaque. The frontier character of the community gave it a unique identity that it shared with other one-industry towns across Canada but, at the same time, identified the community as significantly different from other Ukrainian communities in the larger urban and industrial centres of Canada.

# THE SPIRIT LAKE INTERNMENT CAMP

## 1915-1916

The earliest Ukrainian presence in the Abitibi region dates back to the First World War period. The declaration of the First World War on 15 August, 1914 against Imperial Germany and Austria-Hungary, found several thousand recent Ukrainian immigrants across Canada in a difficult situation. Those who were not naturalized were considered as 'enemy aliens' and they were subject to registration and also, to internment. As soon as the war broke out, the Canadian federal government issued a number of orders-in-council to control the presence of visiting German and Austro-Hungarian military, tourists and travellers in Canada. Among the first who were interned were German and Austrian sailors on ships in the eastern Canadian ports. The number of orders-in-council was gradually increased to include all 'enemy aliens' that is, citizens of Austria-Hungary and Imperial Germany who were living in Canada and somehow came to the attention of the law enforcement authorities. In individual cases, 'enemy aliens' who contravened any orders-in-council, for example, who were found to own firearms, were interned and sent to the internment camps.

Among the internment camps established in various parts of Canada, a camp was created on 13 January, 1915 at Spirit Lake (near Amos, Quebec) to hold enemy aliens, that is, citizens of Austria-Hungary and Imperial Germany. The anti-immigrant attitudes and panic caused by the outbreak of the war contributed to these actions by the federal government. The local Amos businessmen saw the establishment of this camp as a business opportunity that would benefit the colonization of the region. The plans were to use the internees to clear the land and develop an experimental farm to aid in the settlement of this region. The internees were paid twenty-five cents per day to clear the forest. The first internees arrived in January, 1915 in the middle of winter. Many were confused by their internment because they were at first encouraged to immigrate and settle in Canada but now they were treated as 'enemy aliens'. Among the 1,144 'Austrian' prisoners interned at this camp in 1916 were a large number of Galicians or Ukrainians, recent immigrants from Austria-Hungary.[8] The Canadian federal government feared that single and able-bodied male immigrants from Austria-Hungary would attempt to cross the border into the then neutral United States and eventually make their way back through Italy, also neutral at this time, to Austria-Hungary. Once they returned, they would be drafted into their armed forces and participate in the war against the Allies including Canada. To prevent this possibility, many recent immigrants from Austria-Hungary who were without employment, in difficulty with the law or attempting to cross the border into the United States were arrested and interned. In some cases, the wives and families were sent to internment camps at their own request to be with their fathers and husbands because they had no means of support and were destitute in Montreal. In other cases, local and municipal authorities, faced with the costs of assisting unemployed recent immigrants, also arranged for their transfer to the internment camps. According to some sources, the Spirit Lake Camp held 60 families from St. Michael's Ukrainian Catholic Church in Iberville (Montreal).

The internment camp at Spirit Lake was in operation for two years and it was closed in November, 1916. The isolation, the long and bitterly cold winters, the hard physical work outdoors made the internment especially difficult. As a result, the internment was marked by discipline and labour problems. There were several attempts to escape by individual prisoners and one escaped prisoner, Iwan Gregoraszczuk was shot and killed on 7 June, 1915 by a French Canadian farmer near La Sarre. The majority of the 'Austro-Hungarians' were released on parole in 1916 and many were hired by various companies across eastern Canada for work in ship yards, coal mines, and the railways. Some former internees were sent as far as Cape Breton in northern Nova Scotia to work in the steel mills. Former internees from other internment camps were sent to other industrial centres across Canada for work. There is no record of any of the Ukrainian internees continuing to reside in the Abitibi area after their release.[9]

However, this experience of internment in Spirit Lake, as well as in other camps across Canada, left the internees, their families and especially the leadership in the Ukrainian community with an ambivalent and wary attitude towards the Canadian federal government. For them, the policies of the Canadian government were perceived to be not substantially different from those of the authoritarian governments they knew in eastern Europe.[10] In the Ukrainian community, the 'fear of the barbed wire fence' remained among the leadership until the years after the Second World War. The internment experience alienated a substantial portion of the Ukrainian community from the mainstream of Canadian life and marked them in law as well as in the popular mentality not only as foreigners but also as 'enemy aliens'. In several cases, former internees hid the story of their internment from their families and children.[11] For these members of the Ukrainian community, the road towards full integration into Canadian society was particularly difficult.

**The Spirit Lake Internment Camp**, circa 1916.
*Photo credit:* Canadian First World War Internment Recognition Fund

In several internment camps such as Kapuskasing, Ontario, some of the Ukrainian internees formed discussion and political groups that supported the revolutionary events in eastern Europe. They were radicalized by their experiences in the internment camps and when they were released and arrived at urban centres such as Oshawa and Ottawa, they were among the first members of the Ukrainian Labor-Farmer Temple Association and also the Communist Party of Canada in the 1920s. With the establishment of the Soviet Union and especially Soviet Ukraine, a significant percentage of Ukrainian immigrants saw this political development as a realization of their dreams and hopes and became members of the pro-Soviet organizations.[12] These events influenced the formation of Ukrainian political organizations in Canada and also in Quebec.

The story of the internment of Ukrainians during the First World War was generally not included in the popular English-language histories of the Ukrainian Canadian community until the 1980s. Except for a few individuals, the story of the Spirit Lake Internment Camp and the internment of 'enemy aliens' across Canada was not generally known in the Ukrainian community in Val-d'Or.

# THE SHEPTETSKI COLONY

## 1928-1935

In 1925, Father Josephat Jean began preparations to establish a Ukrainian agricultural colony called Sheptetski approximately 40 km. north of Amos, Quebec. Father Jean was an interesting individual, born in Rimouski, Quebec and after he was ordained in the Roman Catholic Church, answered the call to convert to the Greek Catholic Church to minister to the Ukrainian settlers in western Canada. He found himself in Halychyna at the beginning of the First World War where he was sent to learn the Ukrainian language, customs and culture. After the war, he was involved as an interpreter and diplomat in the unsuccessful attempts to establish an independent Ukrainian government. He was also a Chaplain in the Ukrainian Galician Army during the military conflicts. In the early 1920s, Father Jean was a witness in Yugoslavia to attempts by Serbian activists to convert the Ukrainian Greek Catholic Churches to Orthodox Churches and he resisted these efforts. As a result, he was arrested but his status as a British subject prevented further imprisonment and he was released. It was at that time that he returned to Canada.

He realized the need to establish a Ukrainian 'colony' in Canada to welcome Ukrainian refugees and immigrants from the turbulent conditions resulting from the First World War and the succeeding wars in eastern Europe. The colony was intended for Ukrainian immigrants from Yugoslavia and from Halychyna (then western Ukraine under Polish administration). Fr. Jean had examined potential settlement sites in northern Alberta but felt that the Abitibi region had the best prospects. The location was closer to Halifax and Quebec City that were the usual ports for Ukrainian immigrants arriving in Canada in contrast to the long train rides to northern Alberta. In 1926, he began to advertise for settlers for this colony in 'Abitibi' in various Ukrainian periodicals in Canada.[13] He received a large grant of land of 777 square km. from the Quebec provincial government that was surveyed by January, 1927.[14] In Ottawa, the Cabinet awarded a grant of $250.00 by Order-in-Council on 25 June, 1927 to Father Jean 'for hostel to accommodate Ukrainian settlers arriving at proposed settlement at Lake Castagnier, PQ.'[15] The location was named after Metropolitan Andriy Sheptetski (Sheptytsky), head of the Ukrainian Greek Catholic Church in Lviv, Halychyna. In October, 1927, Volodomyr Stepankowski, from the Ukrainian Press Bureau, planned to visit Barraute and meet with Fr. Jean to investigate the settlement project.[16] By November, 1928, he had built a two-storey building approximately 9 metres by 18 metres to serve as a monastery and also, about a dozen houses were built for the prospective new settlers.[17]

In August, 1929, the first two Ukrainian families arrived.[18] In the next year, he began to settle Ukrainian families from Montreal and new arrivals from Europe. He had ambitious plans for this colony as a future center of Ukrainian life in eastern Canada with a Studite Monastery, school, cooperative, Ukrainian library and museum. In other words, Fr. Jean wanted to establish a 'little Ukraine' in Abitibi. However, the isolation of the area, the long winters with deep snows and short growing seasons, and the coming of the Depression in 1929-30 stopped further settlement and limited the arrival of new Ukrainian settlers.[19] Also immigration to Canada was severely curtailed after 1931 because of the Depression and only special categories of immigrants were allowed to enter Canada. In the winter of 1933, Father Jean was assigned to a Ukrainian Catholic parish in Winnipeg[20] and later to Montreal and the colony lost their founder and leader. The pioneers began to leave for other parts of Canada and in 1931 there were only 52 Ukrainians in the colony.[21] Some of the families experienced serious personal economic difficulties and were reduced to poverty through their experiences in the Sheptetski colony. They returned to Montreal, were obliged to live on welfare and became active members of the Ukrainian Orthodox Church.[22]

After 1935, the area was settled by the first French Canadian families mostly from the Montreal area and the settlement was renamed Lac Castagnier.[23] This settlement plan was encouraged by the Quebec provincial government in cooperation with the Roman Catholic Church as a solution to the unemployment problems in the large cities created by the Depression. On 12 April, 1939, a fire destroyed the original building

## THE SHEPTETSKI COLONY (1928-1935)

built by Father Jean as a monastery. With the building, Father Jean's library of rare books from Ukraine was also destroyed.[24] One of the original settlers, Pylyp Andrusyshyn was able to rescue an old Ukrainian Bible that he later donated to the Ukrainian Educational and Cultural Centre in Winnipeg. Many of the French Canadian families left the area after the first winter and the community was gradually depopulated especially after the Second World War. The last few Ukrainian families continued to live and farm in the area until the 1970s.[25] There was only one family left in 1983.[26] Despite the isolation and difficult living conditions, individual Ukrainians sought to make the best of their situation but, as one of the original settlers later stated, they enjoyed the freedom of life on the frontier 'as did the Cossacks in old Ukraine'.

From the mid-1930s, families in the Sheptetski colony maintained close contacts with the growing Ukrainian community in Val-d'Or. In a few cases, families moved to Val-d'Or to contribute to the social and religious life of the community. Also, for historical reasons, the founding of the Sheptetski agricultural colony rather than the opening of the internment camp at Spirit Lake is considered as the origins of the Ukrainian community in Abitibi.

**Wedding Anniversary Celebration,** Lac Castagnier, 1949. *Photo credit:* Stephanie Borsuk MacArthur

## THE ABITIBI GOLD RUSH

### 1923-1939

During the early 1900s, discoveries of mines in Cobalt and in other parts of northern Ontario, led prospectors to extend their search along the Canadian Shield and into northwestern Quebec along the geological formation, the Cadillac-Bouzan Fault. The building of the railways in northern Ontario and Quebec opened the region to mine exploration. According to some reports, many of the railway workers were immigrants from eastern Europe including Ukrainians from western Ukraine who were hired either in Montreal to work into north-western Quebec or in Fort William/Port Arthur to work into north-eastern Ontario. Following the completion of the National Transcontinental Railway line through northwestern Quebec in 1911, prospectors advanced up the Harricana River from Amos to what is today the Val-d'Or region. Among the first mines discovered in this area was the Siscoe Gold Mines Limited, incorporated in 1923. It was established by a small group of Polish miners led by Stanley Siscoe (Stanislaw Szyszka), a Polish immigrant who arrived in Cobalt in 1908. The Siscoe Gold Mine produced the first gold ingot in 1929 and news that the new mine was owned by a Polish immigrant, soon spread among other East European immigrants desperate in search of work following the outbreak of the Depression in October, 1929. A few of the first Ukrainians in this region worked at the Siscoe Gold Mine located on Siscoe Island. The region was informally known as the 'Siscoe area' and the designations Val-d'Or and Bourlamaque became popular after 1935.

This discovery was primary stimulus for the 'Abitibi Gold Rush' that peaked in the mid-1930s in the midst of the Depression. Individual Ukrainian prospectors were part of this 'Gold Rush' and staked the first claims in northeastern Ontario and northwestern Quebec. Among these prospectors were the brothers, Ivan and Mykhailo Matviiv who were known as Jack and Michael Matthews. Not much is known about the early years of the Matthews brothers in Ukraine and in Canada. Since Michael Matthews was born in Ulaszkiwci (now Ukraine) on November

21, 1883,²⁷ it can be assumed that his brother, John was also born in Ulaszkiwci. However, on a passport application made in the 1930s, John claimed that he was born about 1887 in Blind River, Ontario.²⁸ Michael Matthews came to Canada about 1907 and John may have arrived also at that time or later. His obituary states that John had about one year of school and he ran away from home at 14 years old. In Canada, he worked as a miner for fifty cents a day during the winter and prospected in the summers. An old prospector taught him how to read and write.

The next reference to the Matthews brothers was in the spring of 1931 when they staked a claim in Pascalis Township, east of the present site of Val-d'Or. This property was optioned to Noranda Mines. In 1932, Noranda Mines did some diamond drilling in the area. This option was allowed to lapse and the claims were then optioned to Alex Perron of

Mining village of Bourlamaque, 1935
These small houses were built for newly arrived miners during the spring of 1935

Kirkland Lake, Ontario. The claims were incorporated in June, 1932 as the Matthews Gold Mines Limited.²⁹ Alex Perron purchased the property from the Matthews brothers in 1933 and the Perron Gold Mine was established in 1934. The mine began production on 20 February, 1936. The exact amount that the Matthews brothers received from Alex Perron for the sale of the mine is not known. Through their prospecting, the Matthews brothers contributed to the prosperity of Val-d'Or during the Depression. John Matthews travelled to Halychyna (now western Ukraine) where he married Stephanie Powlyisyn, a teacher, and returned with her to Canada, arriving on 27 August, 1934. On the passenger list,

John claimed that he had $60,000.00 in his possession.[30] The Matthews brothers moved to Oshawa in the late 1930s and continued to prospect across Canada including the Arctic regions. During the years 1940-1951, John Matthews prospected in the Opemiska district in Quebec, the North West Territories, Alaska and the Arctic. According to one report, he crossed the Bering Sea in a canoe and prospected on the Russian side in Siberia. John later founded Bulldog Gold Mines in Yellowknife and was a Director of Bulldog Gold Mines. He was a member of the Prospectors and Mine Developers Association.[31] John Matthews was known as the 'Big Yanko' because he always wore a ten-gallon Texas-style hat and loud plaid shirts. He was well known in Yellowknife, Val-d'Or and Cobalt and travelled throughout the world. In Canadian mining circles, he was recognized as a 'millionaire' and a colourful figure. John died at age 71 years in Toronto. The Matthews brothers were among the better known Ukrainian prospectors in the Val-d'Or region.

Prospecting increased after gold prices rose from $20.67 an ounce to $35.00 an ounce in 1934 on the international money market.[32] In 1936, mines were exempted from paying taxes for the first three years. In the Val-d'Or and Malartic area, a large number of mines were opened: Siscoe Gold Mine poured the first gold ingot in 1929; Sullivan Consolidated Mines and East Malartic Mines began production in 1934; Canadian Malartic Mines, Lamaque Mines and Sigma Mines began production in 1935; Sladen Malartic in 1938; Golden Manitou in 1941 and East Sullivan in 1944.

The finance capital to build and operate most of these mines came from the large metropolitan centers of Montreal and especially Toronto with direct links with investors from the United States. In almost all cases, the Boards of Directors of these holding companies included one member who was a resident of the United States. The mining technology in use at that time was largely of American design. The manufacturing of the mining machinery and equipment was done in the United States or by American subsidiaries in Canada. Along with the American technology came American mining methods and systems and of course, American mining specialists.[33]

Many of the first mining engineers were Americans or Canadians who received their mining education in the United States. When the mines were being established, these engineers brought specialized and technical workers with previous mining experience in the United States and in other parts of Canada. During the building of the Lamaque mine, the construction company brought their own carpenters from Toronto to build the shaft and main buildings. Among these workers were three or four Ukrainians. Since the mining boom occurred during the Depression, there was no shortage of unskilled labour.

During the first years of the mining boom in the 1930s, travel to the Val-d'Or and Bourlamaque region was especially difficult due to the geography of the area. Travel by bush planes was possible but expensive and at the mercy of the weather. In summer, floatplanes flew from Rouyn-Noranda. In winter, planes equipped with skis landed on the ice-covered local lakes. In the Val-d'Or and Malartic area, the Harricana River connecting with the railway at Amos provided the only route by which supplies, labour and mining equipment came into the region by riverboats and barges. In the winter, supplies and people travelled by horse and dog sled over 'winter roads', that is, across frozen lakes and rivers. By the end of 1937, a gravel road was built to link with Amos so that the Val-d'Or camp was no longer isolated in the fall freeze-up and spring break-up seasons.[34] The building of this road made the riverboats obsolete. They were drydocked by the Thomson River Bridge for many years.

# THE SECOND WAVE OF UKRAINIAN IMMIGRATION TO CANADA

### 1924-1939

The large majority of Ukrainians who arrived in the Val-d'Or-Bourlamaque region were from the second wave of Ukrainian immigration that arrived in Canada during the years 1924-1939. Approximately 70,000 Ukrainians arrived during these years from Halychyna, Volyn and Bukovyna (now western Ukraine). This wave of immigration was the result of revolution, civil war and insurrection in Ukraine, more particularly in western Ukraine, which fell under Polish administration after 1920.[35] Many were witnesses to these events and some were former soldiers from the armies of the Ukrainian National Republic that fought against the Soviets and also against the Polish military. Some of the Ukrainian veterans continued to consider themselves as still 'on active service' and were militant nationalists. The new immigrants brought with them this legacy of political and cultural antagonism between Ukrainians and Poles and continued the political struggles between the nationalists and pro-Soviets. In the Ukrainian Canadian community, the Cold War began in the early 1920s.

By the 1920s, Ukrainian settlers who arrived in Canada prior to the First World War as part of the first wave of immigration, began to form local, regional and national associations to reflect the various and often conflicting religious and political interests of the many segments of the community. The second wave of Ukrainian immigration after the First World War was met by a growing network of community associations and organizations built by the first wave of immigrants. Individuals either contributed to this development by joining existing organizations or by creating their own community structures for their specific needs and requirements. In some cases, they became members of the pro-communist or pro-nationalist community depending on who first met them when they arrived in particular centres in Canada and introduced them to the organized Ukrainian community.

# THE SECOND WAVE OF UKRAINIAN IMMIGRATION TO CANADA (1924-1939)

Most of these first Ukrainians immigrated to western Canada in the years 1926-30 as farm labourers or railway workers. The Ukrainians were recruited by agents of railway and steamship companies in the small villages of western Ukraine. This region fell under Polish administration after the First World War and economic opportunities for the young Ukrainian males were extremely limited. Some immigrants left their families and farms behind in western Ukraine in the hope of establishing themselves before bringing their families over. Others came in the hope of earning enough money and then returning to their home villages in western Ukraine to buy more land and establishing themselves as large-scale farmers. In many cases, the Ukrainians sold part of their land or borrowed money at high interest rates to pay for their travel to Canada.

Some of the more fortunate farm labourers found work with friends and relatives who came and established themselves during the first wave of immigration in 1891-1914. Others found work on farms especially during the harvest seasons and also on railways. Others claimed homesteads in western Canada but soon realized that clearing the land for farming was an enormous physical effort and sold or abandoned their farms especially after the Depression began in 1929. During the Depression years, most Ukrainian farm labourers who, only a few years earlier were encouraged to immigrate to Canada, found themselves unwanted and unemployed. They had to compete for what little work there was available with Canadian-born workers. Without the knowledge of the English or French languages, the popular culture and without naturalized status, they were at a particular disadvantage. They sought assistance and comfort from fellow immigrants and extended their search for work through formal and informal networks of friends and acquaintances. They accepted any jobs that were available on the farms, railroads and in the forests. In some cases, their payment for work on farms was only room and board. The Ukrainian immigrants pushed their search for jobs, any jobs, to all parts of Canada including the frontier mining communities such as Val-d'Or.

Many of the Ukrainian immigrants tended to interpret their difficult experiences in Canada in terms of Ukrainian politics. Some sought to improve their situation by turning to social and political action while others sought to raise the status and prestige of their community. Those who sought social and political action supported the growing Ukrainian communist movement in Canada that eagerly sought their membership while the others joined the Ukrainian nationalist organizations. The nationalist organizations attempted to raise the status and prestige of the Ukrainians both within the community and among the larger Canadian community. They sought to influence the Canadian government through democratic political activities. Through their political activities, the Canadian government knew that the Ukrainian nationalists in Canada were also hostile to the Polish government that administered Halychyna (Galicia) and the government sought to control and limit public manifestations of Ukrainian nationalism. This antagonism to the Polish administration, reinforced the rivalry between the pro-communists and nationalists that remained the main competing opposition movements in the community.

The question of support or opposition to Soviet Ukraine and the Soviet Union was the deciding factor in determining the allegiance of individuals and organizations in the Ukrainian community in Val-d'Or and Bourlamaque. This division influenced in a fundamental way the evolution of the Ukrainian community in Val-d'Or and Bourlamaque and the Ukrainian Canadian community as a whole. These two tendencies inevitably clashed and splintered the Ukrainian community.[36]

# THE EARLY YEARS

## 1933-1939

In their search for employment, the Ukrainian immigrants relied on personal contacts and networks of friends and acquaintances. Rumours of job openings would result in periodic rushes to particular localities. When the mines began to open in the Val-d'Or region, persons seeking work would travel by train to Amos and from there take riverboats to the wharf at the Sullivan mine site. From Sullivan, they would make their way, sometimes on foot, to the Siscoe, Lamaque and other mine sites. They would arrive at the mine gates hoping to be hired by mine management. Among this group were the first Ukrainians miners. Since most were unskilled labourers, they would apply to work underground which also was the most difficult and dangerous work.[37]

**Ukrainian Family Picnic at Blouin Lake, 1938.**
Among those present were members of the Sweryd, Barylo, Lenyk, Zownir, Soya, Dubik and other families. Blouin Lake was a popular picnic site for all members of the Ukrainian community in Val-d'Or-Bourlamaque for many decades. Various fundraising events were held at the lake during the Second World War. By 1950, all these families left Val-d'Or for other parts of Canada. *Photo credit:* Stephanie Borsuk MacArthur

In the mid-1930s, Val-d'Or-Bourlamaque had all the characteristics of a frontier mining camp. There was only one street, later Third Avenue. In the typical mining-camp tradition, movie theatres and hotels were built before there were sidewalks and a sewage system. There was a great shortage of houses and living quarters. The town of Bourlamaque was officially founded on 20 April, 1934.[38] The Lamaque mine management had hoped to establish Bourlamaque as a company town.[39] In 1935, fifty-three log cabins were built at the Lamaque town site for the miners and they are today a historic site. At the same time, the townsite with streets was laid out by the mining company and in October, 1936, plans were made to build the Bourlamaque Hotel, operated by a subsidiary company. Plans were also made to build a movie theatre.[40] The mining camp did not have a cemetery and recent deaths from various causes were usually buried in Rouyn-Noranda or other towns. At the Library and Archives Canada in Ottawa, there is a photograph of a young boy of approximately 5-6 years old who passed away in 1935 and who was described as a Ukrainian. There is no record of his burial in Val-d'Or and he may have been buried elsewhere.[41] According to available information, the first Ukrainian male child born in the Val-d'Or area was Jerry Roman Zownir who was born in 1936 on Siscoe Island. He may have been the first child of European origin born there also.[42]

Miners who objected to the restrictions and limitations of a company town, lived outside the mine townsite in the 'camp' which later became the town of Val-d'Or.[43] The mining camp was a collection of log houses, tar-paper shacks and many hotels. Ivan Lenyk, one of the first Ukrainian pioneers and his family had to spend their first winter in a one-room 'dug-out' built of logs and covered with earth on the corner of 4th Avenue and 14th street.[44] The camp was incorporated as the village of Val d'Or on 15 August, 1935. The name, Val d'Or (the Valley of Gold) was selected by a few resident French Canadian businessmen to express some optimism in the midst of the Depression. The town was incorporated as a town on 17 May, 1937. The first municipal administration was established[45] and by this time, electric power was available to the residents. By October, 1936, the municipal council issued contracts to build a water and sewer system.⁴⁶ Construction began on a Roman Catholic Church for the growing population estimated at 2,000 in Val-d'Or and 5,000 in the region.⁴⁷ Recent immigrants formed a large percentage of the population in the early years. According to some contemporary accounts, there were approximately 200-300 Ukrainians in a population of over 4,000 by 1938.⁴⁸ Bourlamaque was viewed as an 'English' locality while Val-d'Or was predominantly 'French'. ⁴⁹

Individual Ukrainians with some financial resources attempted to take advantage of the housing shortage to build boarding houses and bunkhouses. Others established restaurants, stores and businesses to cater to the miners.⁵⁰ Mike Sorokowski arrived in Val-d'Or in 1933 and built a log cabin where he operated one of the first provision stores in the area. He later established a general store in the mining village, Perron.⁵¹ Ukrainian miners sought out friends and acquaintances from other parts of Canada or fellow villagers from their home areas in Ukraine. The same pattern of forming friendships and associations was followed by other ethnocultural groups. For example, the Slovaks organized Branch 12 of the Canadian Slovak League in 1936.

It was such a small group of Ukrainian miners from Kirkland Lake who were members of the Workers Benevolent Association of Canada (WBA), a pro-communist association, that met in a private home and held their first meeting. In May, 1936, there were twelve members in the WBA branch.⁵² The frontier environment of Val-d'Or, the primitive working conditions at the mines, lack of living accommodations, the high cost of living, the anti-union attitudes of mine management and the continuing Depression in the rest of Canada increased the appeal of this small group of Ukrainian pro-communists. In a short time, these Ukrainians were able to claim a significant following among the Ukrainian community in Val-d'Or. In November, 1935, they rented a room from one of their members for $25.00 per month where they held dances and other fund-raising activities.⁵³

Other Ukrainians reacted strongly to the growing pro-communist presence and decided to counter their influence. This small group of Ukrainian nationalists included some veterans of the armed forces of the

Ukrainian National Republic of 1918-20. They maintained contacts with each other and with other Ukrainian nationalist groups in other parts of Canada through personal correspondence and through the Ukrainian nationalist newspapers. On 9 February, 1936, twelve men and one woman met in a private home and decided to formally establish a branch of the Ukrainian National Federation (UNF), a Ukrainian pro-nationalist organization. They elected an executive and planned a series of political and social meetings.[54]

**UNF Hall**, View from 4th Avenue, circa 1939. *Photo credit:* Stephanie Borsuk MacArthur

The Ukrainian National Federation was established as a national organization in Edmonton in 1932 by members of the Ukrainian War Veterans Association in Canada. The new organization sought to mobilize all members of the Ukrainian community in support of the cause of Ukrainian independence in Europe.[55]

Because of the severe shortage of accommodations and housing, all organizational events were held in private homes. The new UNF branch established a three-member press committee to raise funds for the Press Fund and encourage subscribers to the newspaper, *Novy Shliakh (New Pathway)*. They continued to meet and hold dances and communal suppers in private homes. Three dances were held to raise funds to help build the local French Canadian Roman Catholic Church.[56] The first dance ended in a fight between the nationalists and communists. The nationalists sought assistance from the Roman Catholic parish priest who advised them to report the incident to the local detachment of the Royal Canadian Mounted Police (RCMP). At the second dance, there were no problems because of the police presence.[57] In July, 1936, they decided to rent a room in the home of one of their members for $50.00 a month. During the first year of organized activity in 1936, there were twelve meetings and minutes were kept. Funds were also raised for the Ukrainian Liberation Fund and for Ukrainian war invalids.[58]

The local branch of the WBA also devoted their efforts to fundraising for various Ukrainian pro-communist newspapers and the funds were regularly collected and sent to Winnipeg, the headquarters of the Ukrainian pro-communist movement in Canada.[59] The Val-d'Or Branch belonged to the Timmins District of WBA. In May, 1936, the Val-d'Or WBA had twelve members and they cooperated with the local Croatian and Russian left-wing groups in organizing social and political events. This small WBA Branch spent much time and effort in promoting their cause among the Ukrainian miners in Val-d'Or and Bourlamaque but in November, 1936, they reported that among the over 200 Ukrainians, there were only 26 subscribers to their press.[60]

At this time, a branch of the Ukrainian Labor Farmer Temple Association (ULFTA) was also established. The ULFTA was affiliated with the WBA and many members were also members of the WBA. They followed a pro-communist policy and were opposed to the Ukrainian nationalist groups. The ULFTA faced the same problems as other Ukrainian organizations mainly, the isolation of this frontier town from other Ukrainian centers. For example, the Timmins District had written four letters in October, 1936 before they received a reply from the Val-d'Or Branch.[61] According to one report, there were up to 500 Ukrainians in the Val-d'Or region and an additional 500 Ukrainians in the Rouyn-Noranda area. The cost of living was very high and according to visitors from Montreal, some Ukrainian miners were accused of living beyond their means.[62]

The annual meeting of the UNF branch was held on 24 January, 1937 and fifteen members were present. On 21 February, 1937 in the presence of Wasyl Voinarivsky, the UNF organizer for Eastern Canada, a lot was purchased to build a hall. Ivan Michael Lenyk had purchased a lot to build a store on 4th Avenue between the 14th and 15th Streets. He was able to obtain permission from the local civic authorities to divide this lot and he then sold the eastern portion to the local branch of the UNF.[63] In March, a building committee was established. Almost every month, there were dances, social evenings, lectures and other events at which donations were solicited for the building of the new hall. Community suppers were held on Ukrainian Christmas and Easter. Draws were held to raise funds for the nationalist press and purchase nationalist literature for their library. The hall was built with volunteer labour under the direction of Ukrainian carpenters who were brought from Toronto to build the shaft and other structures at the Lamaque Mine. The UNF hall was completed on 3 December, 1937 on the corner of 4th Avenue and 15th Street. An official opening was held on 12 December with a dance in the evening. The hall served as a clubhouse, cultural center and church for visiting Ukrainian Orthodox and Catholic clergy. The hall had a small stage, a canteen and a cloakroom. In the basement were the washrooms, storage rooms and a kitchen with a large wood-fired stove that was used to prepare the various communal suppers and banquets.

The completion of the hall by the UNF was important in their political rivalry with the local pro-communist groups by attracting and retaining members. Some Ukrainians who were generally apolitical were first attracted by the social and cultural events at the hall and over time became involved in the political activities of the branch. The building of the UNF Hall was also good business for Ivan Lenyk because he had the monopoly on selling beer and other refreshments at the hall. Despite the lack of any knowledge and experience, he also opened a small 'pharmacy' where he sold various drugs and medicines. He operated this 'pharmacy' until the town received municipal status and a provincial inspector obliged him to close this part of his store.

During 1937, there were eleven UNF meetings and two special meetings. The special meetings were called to elect new executive members when there were resignations due to departures and changes in work schedules. The mines worked on the shift system which meant that some members were absent for weeks. This problem of high turnover was typical of the Ukrainian organizations in other one-industry towns at this time and reflected the unstable frontier conditions of the community. Through the examination of the UNF branch minutes, it is quickly obvious that some members were especially active. For example, one member of the executive prepared and gave fifteen speeches and lectures in one year.

The UNF branch was also visited by organizers from their headquarters in Winnipeg who spoke on the current Ukrainian political issues. A delegate was sent to the Annual UNF Convention in Toronto and he paid his own expenses. During the early years, delegates from the Val-d'Or branch regularly attended the Annual UNF Conventions in the larger cities.

The Ukrainian nationalist movement suffered a serious blow when Col. Evhen Konovalets, the leader of the Organization of Ukrainian Nationalists, was assassinated by a Soviet agent on May 23, 1938 in Rotterdam.[64] His death led to a competition to succeed him for the leadership of the Ukrainian nationalist movement that split the movement at a crucial time in Ukrainian history. A fund-raising campaign was initiated in Canada in his memory and contributions were made from Val-d'Or.[65]

In the UNF, attempts were made to organize a drama group, a choir and a Ukrainian school 'Ridna Shkola'. There were sixteen children under twelve years old at the commemoration of the 20th anniversary of the declaration of independence of the Western Ukrainian Republic held on 13 November, 1938. It was generally acknowledged that there was a deficiency in the level of cultural-educational work and a member agreed to read out loud from the Ukrainian nationalist press and publications for other members. Fund-raising for various nationalist causes was one of the main activities of the branch throughout the years.[66]

The political events in central Europe surrounding the emergence of Carpatho-Ukraine (with the breakup of Czechoslovakia) in 1938-39 raised hopes among the nationalists that a Ukrainian state would be formed. Some nationalists hoped that Germany under Adolph Hitler would re-draw the map of central and eastern Europe to the benefit of a nationalist Ukraine. The suppression of this nascent Carpatho-Ukrainian government by the Hungarian armed forces in the spring of 1939 obliged many Ukrainian nationalists in Canada and in Europe to reevaluate their political position in regards to Germany and her allies.

A women's branch of the UNF, the Organization of Ukrainian Canadian Women (OYK) was formed on 30 May, 1938[67] and a youth section, the Ukrainian National Youth Federation (MUN) was founded on 24 December, 1939.[68] The women's group was traditionally responsible for the most important work in the hall, that is, preparing the various social events including communal suppers and banquets. The local UNF Drama Group performed in Rouyn and was well received. The new Drama Group was especially active and performed several plays that attracted spectators and new members to the branch.

**20th Anniversary of the November, 1918 Uprising in Lviv.** Commemoration held at the UNF Hall on 13 November, 1938 in Val-d'Or

By the end of 1938, the annual cycle of cultural and political events was well established and served as a barometer of the life and activity of the UNF branch. In January, a Christmas Eve Supper was held; on 22 January, Ukrainian Independence Day; in April, Taras Shevchenko Memorial Concert and Easter Supper. In the fall, the November Memorial Day was commemorated and in December, a St. Nicholas Concert was held. During the year, there were also dances, social evenings, plays and picnics. In a few individual cases, miners were able to sponsor their wives from western Ukraine, which added to the celebrations and the small but growing number of Ukrainian families. In one case, Frank Moskal returned in 1936 to his native village, Trebyshiw, Bukovyna, to reunite with his family. He had arrived in Canada in 1929 leaving a young wife and two sons in Bukovyna. He worked as a miner at Lamaque Mine from 1934. However, due to some misunderstandings, he could not persuade his wife to return with him to Val-d'Or and he returned alone. He continued to live in Val-d'Or, married again and worked at the mine until 1968.[69] 'Going-away' parties were held for members who left for other parts of Canada and, in one case, for a member who returned with

**UNF Drama Group**, Trip to Rouyn-Noranda, 1940
*Photo credit:* Stefanie Borsuk MacArthur

his family to western Ukraine. Despite the restrictions on immigration to Canada, some Ukrainians did immigrate during the Depression years. For example, Peter and Julia Mudry immigrated to Saskatchewan in 1936 from Halychyna and farmed. But after four years of farming and severe drought, Peter moved his family to Val-d'Or, to work in the gold mines. They stayed for only six months and moved to Toronto.[70]

Despite this activity, there were signs of problems with discipline and decline in interest among members. The UNF School Committee requested more parental involvement, meetings were missed and schedules were not maintained. Membership was withdrawn from one member and another member was suspended for six months for rowdy behavior at meetings and social events in the hall.[71]

Among the Ukrainian pro-communist community, an annual cycle of social and political events was also established. These commemorated revolutionary events and holidays in addition to plays, concerts and social events. A Women's Section of the ULFTA with seven members was established.[72] In May, 1937, a committee of three members was elected to aid their countrymen in the Lemko region in eastern Poland. Funds were raised for the Canadian volunteers in the International Brigades in Spain. A significant indicator of the level of political commitment among some members was the fact that several Ukrainian volunteers from Val-d'Or left in 1937 to serve in Spain in the International Brigades.[73]

By the end of 1937, the Ukrainian miners were beginning to put down permanent roots in Val-d'Or. Many of the miners lived in the company town of Bourlamaque. Others bought lots with the intention to build houses. There were three grocery stores and one restaurant owned by local Ukrainians. There was also a store in Bourlamaque that sold Ukrainian newspapers. However, the town remained very much a frontier mining community. One pro-communist correspondent complained that many Ukrainian workers were not class conscious, did not read their newspapers and were not interested in organizational work. The ULFTA branch also formed a Press Committee to encourage subscribers and contributors of articles on Val-d'Or to the press. The local branch also received visits from organizers from the national headquarters in Winnipeg that spoke on current political issues.[74]

The Young Communist League (YCL) whose membership included members from all ethnocultural groups, attempted to organize a meeting at the Palace Theatre in January, 1937. The local Roman Catholic clergy opposed this meeting and the Palace Theatre refunded the YCL organizers their deposit.[75] It is interesting to note that the Palace Theatre was built by Dimitri Chalykoff, an immigrant from Bulgaria, who was also Mayor of Val-d'Or in 1937.

One main difficulty in organizing events among the ULFTA members was due to the fact that there were no Ukrainian teachers. They were eventually able to obtain the services of a volunteer and a school was opened. An attempt to organize a choir was unsuccessful because of shift work and lack of discipline. Also, a major complaint was the lack of a hall or meeting place where they could hold their rehearsals.[76]

There were also political problems. In Montreal, the anti-communist 'Red Squad' from the Quebec Provincial Police raided the ULFTA hall on St. Lawrence Boulevard on January 26, 1938 under the provisions of the Padlock Law.[77] This law "... forbade citizens to use [a house] or allow any person to make use of it to propagate Communism or Bolshevism by any means whatsoever". In Val-d'Or, there was the constant threat of the police interfering with their activities. At a meeting held on 30 April, 1938, there were 20 men and 3 women. There were also four Quebec Provincial Policemen and two detectives. One detective (obviously of Ukrainian origin) took notes of all that was said. The purpose of the meeting was to organize a branch of the Association to Aid the Liberation Movement in Western Ukraine. No one signed the membership list because of the police presence.[78] In August, an organizer visited Val-d'Or and a branch of 30 members was eventually organized.[79] Despite these obstacles, the Communist Party of Canada (CPC) signed 16 new members by April, 1938 in Val-d'Or.[80]

In spite of these and other difficulties, social and political events were organized by the ULFTA, an orchestra was formed and concerts were performed locally. Also Ukrainian dancing was taught and a sewing circle was established. In September, 1938, there were reports in the press that plans were underway to build a ULFTA hall in Val-d'Or.[81] In October, a branch of the Association to Aid the Liberation Movement in Western Ukraine was formed in Malartic and in January, 1939, a Youth Club was established.[82]

The Ukrainian left-wing organizations cooperated with other ethnocultural groups in their fund-raising and other activities. At that time, there was a [Russian] Maxim Gorky Club, Finnish Workers Club, Malartic Progressive Group, a Croatian organization and an English Branch.[83] The Val D'Or Youth Orchestra travelled to Rouyn and Kirkland Lake and performed to raise funds for the building of the hall.[84] In October, a bazaar was held to raise funds.[85] By December, a lot was purchased and plans were made to start building their hall.[86]

The completion of the railway to Val-d'Or in November, 1938, greatly facilitated travel and communications with other Ukrainian communities in Quebec and across Canada. Some Ukrainian workers had also worked on the building of the railway.[87] There were road communications with Amos and also with Rouyn and northeastern Ontario but there was still no all-weather road communications with Montreal and Ottawa.[88]

In March, 1939, a ULFTA Youth Branch was organized in Val-d'Or and the Women's Section of the ULFTA had eleven members.[89] Some events such as the Taras Shevchenko Concert were held in the Finnish Hall on 11th Street in Val d'Or. In April, a memorial service was held in Val-d'Or for two volunteers, Andrew Sich and John Lukasevich, who were killed in Spain while serving with the International Brigades.[90] In June, 1939, an orchestra from Toronto played at a local theatre as part of their Eastern Canadian tour.[91] News from Europe about the conclusion of the Hitler-Stalin Pact on 23 August, 1939, no doubt, disillusioned some members but according to press reports, the ULFTA branch continued its activities. The signing of this Pact gave Nazi Germany the assurance to attack Poland without the fear of an attack from the Soviet Union. Nazi Germany invaded Poland on 1 September, 1939 and the Soviet Union occupied eastern Poland a few weeks later.

# THE SECOND WORLD WAR

## 1939-1945

The outbreak of the Second World War in September, 1939, did have a significant effect on the development of mining in Canada in general and on the Ukrainian community in Val-d'Or. The need for increased gold production became urgent to pay for war supplies and armaments from the United States and correct the balance of payments. In 1940, gold in Canada was valued at $38.50 an ounce because of the devaluation of the Canadian dollar.[92] Gold mining was designated by the federal government as an 'essential' war industry and given priority in the availability of manpower and material.[93] Despite the increase in the value of gold, miners in Val-d'Or received $4.75 per day while in Ontario, miners received $5.20 per day.[94] During the first year of the Second World War, there was still some unemployment among Ukrainians and others kept leaving and arriving in search of work. Individual Ukrainians travelled to the larger urban centers to join various branches of the Canadian armed forces.[95]

The occupation of eastern Poland (western Ukraine and Belorus) by the Soviet Army in September, 1939 created a particularly difficult political and military problem for the British Empire and also Canada. For all practical purposes, the Soviet Union was perceived as a partner if not an ally, of Nazi Germany, and it was not impossible that the British Empire and Canada could also be at war with the Soviet Union. At the national level, the Communist Party of Canada and the ULFTA followed the political direction of the Soviet Union that claimed that this was an 'imperialist war' because both sides in this conflict were known as 'enemies' of the Soviet Union. In some cases, individual CPC members distributed leaflets in the larger urban centres advising Canadians not to volunteer for service in the Canadian military.

In Val-d'Or, the Soviet occupation of eastern Poland led to the disbandment of the Association for the Defence of Western Ukraine and its local branches in Val-d'Or and Malartic in November, 1939.[96]

The local ULFTA branch, however, continued to campaign on miners' issues and appeals were made to the local Ukrainian miners to join the International Mine Mill and Smelter Workers Union, a pro-communist union.[97] Fundraising activities continued and in January, 1940, the sum of $325.00 was raised for the Press Fund. This amount was raised despite the fact that the ULFTA did not have their own building, operated under the Padlock Law and had many young and inexperienced members.[98]

In January, 1940, the Royal Canadian Mounted Police (RCMP) began its regular surveillance of the Ukrainian left-wing community in the Val-d'Or region. This surveillance began with 'discrete inquiries' and the monitoring of the postal mailbox rented by the local ULFTA branch.[99]

The war also had an impact on other ethnocultural communities in Val-d'Or. The Soviet Union attacked Finland in November, 1939 and this led to the First Winter War. Funds and supplies were raised across Canada to aid Finland and individual volunteers began to travel to Finland to enlist in the Finnish Army. At least four Finns from Val-d'Or volunteered to serve in the Finnish American Legion.[100]

In the Ukrainian nationalist community, activities continued as before. As the war industries began to develop and expand in other parts of Canada, some miners left to find work in the manufacturing centres in southern Ontario. During this period, some of the most active members left and a decline in membership, activities and interest was noticed.[101] The Ukrainian school, Ridna Shkola that had 16 students, was obliged to cease its activities because of the lack of teachers.

Although there was growth in the local municipal services, the living and working conditions in Val-d'Or did not improve substantially with the outbreak of the war. There was also the ever-present danger of accidents in the local mines. On 8 March, 1940, two Ukrainian miners were killed in mine accidents in Malartic.[102] They were members of the local ULFTA and their deaths no doubt encouraged others to seek better opportunities in the expanding war industries in other parts of Canada.

The departure of the more active members of the Ukrainian organizations contributed to the general low level of political activity. Attempts were made by the ULFTA to educate the Ukrainian miners about

# THE SECOND WORLD WAR (1939-1945)

**Children outside Ukrainian Hall**, June 7, 1941
Children were the participants in the Patriotic Parade organized by UNF.

current political issues. On 1 March, 1940 a larger hall was rented and a school was started to teach English however, there was general apathy. A ULFTA lecture series was begun but few came due to shiftwork and finding a suitable meeting place.[103]

The RCMP surveillance reports, however, provided a more active picture of the left-wing community. According to the RCMP, the local Communist Party of Canada and the ULFTA branch in Val-d'Or were essentially the same organization. The ULFTA was described as '... fairly well organized and supported. Either meeting or classes for the young people are held nearly every evening in their [rented] hall at 584-3$^{rd}$ Avenue ... This hall is on the ground floor of a building ...' A list of members or sympathizers was included with the report. The RCMP report added, 'It is reported further that a large percentage of the Ukrainians at Val d'Or, PQ are off and on followers of this organization.'[104]

On 4 June, 1940, the Communist Party of Canada and several other affiliated organizations including the ULFTA were banned by the

51

Canadian federal government and their assets were confiscated. Most of the leadership of the ULFTA was arrested and interned. They were held with the other leaders of the Communist Party in Kananiskis, Alberta, Camp Petawawa in Ontario and later in the Hull Jail in Hull (now Gatineau, Quebec). In Val-d'Or, the lot for their proposed hall was seized and their organizational activities were suspended. The WBA, a fraternal society with branches in Val-d'Or and Malartic, was not banned but was forbidden to accept new members. The RCMP report noted that '... All Aliens of European extraction according to public opinion are [politically] unreliable'.[105]

The local UNF branch continued its yearly cycle of activities. A mandolin orchestra was formed. The new executive for 1941 included eleven positions from head (Holova) to manager (Hospodar) of the hall. In the 1941 census, the general population of Val-d'Or and Bourlamaque included 5,930 individuals composed of the following major groups:

**Patriotic Parade in support of the British War Effort by UNF members**, 7 June, 1941.
*From left to right:* Wasyl Poremski, Nick Lesiuk, unidentified.
Banner reads *"Onward for Complete British Victory"*. *Photo credit:* Stephanie Borsuk MacArthur

| | |
|---|---:|
| British | 978 |
| French Canadian | 3,588 |
| European[106] | 1,323 |
| Other | 41 |
| **Total** | **5,930** |

According to these statistics, over one-quarter of the population was of European origin. There were at least 284 Ukrainians among the European population.[107] There were 70 Ukrainians in Malartic, 19 in Duparquet[108], 9 in Cadillac and 134 in the remainder of the county including Lac Castagnier and Perron. In examining detailed census statistics for the Abitibi region, at least 516 individuals gave 'Ukrainian' as their racial origin. From these statistics, it can be concluded that there were more 'Europeans' than 'British' in Val-d'Or and therefore, there was not the 'critical mass' as in larger urban centres that created the conditions and the pressure for rapid assimilation into the Anglophone community. The local French Canadian community did not express much interest in 'assimilating' the East European immigrants.

The RCMP report confirmed that leading local members of the Communist Party continued their illegal activities. At this time, Personal History Files were opened by the RCMP on some of the more active members. Although the RCMP felt that there were sufficient grounds for search and possible prosecution of individuals, it was recommended that such action would only drive the local Communist Party organization further underground and thereby making it difficult to obtain information. Lists of prominent CPC members were compiled and the RCMP report added, 'These fellows are the first instigators and they are fully responsible for the subversive communistic and anti-democratic and therefore anti-canadian feelings which is quite evident among the foreign born miners in Val d'Or.'[109] The RCMP reports stated that in Val-d'Or, '... the communists and their sympathizers are strongly concentrated there. Practically every four out of five foreign-born miners in Val d'Or are communists. They are living in Val d'Or and work in mines closely, namely in Sigma Mine, Lamaque Mine and Siscoe Mine...

Ukrainians, they are the strongest; Before the Communist Party became illegal, the Ukrainians in Val d'Or had a strong branch of the ULFTA, Communist Party Ukrainian branch and Ukrainian Communist Youth Federation... Since the Communist Party and the ULFTA became illegal the Ukrainian communists in Val d'Or never gave up their subversive activities however and have been meeting secretly in small groups in private houses of their most trusted members especially on Sundays between 3:00 and 6:00 p.m. Beside holding secret meetings in the above mentioned houses, the Ukrainian and Russian communists are very active in spreading their nefarious bolshevik propaganda around mines and while gathering in wash-rooms, rooming houses where they live. There is a special meeting place, a restaurant called Chicago restaurant ... where the communists congregate very strongly. Practically every evening that place is full of Bolsheviks ...'[110]

Ukrainians in Val-d'Or made the news in Toronto when it was reported in the *Toronto Star* that Mike Baraniuk shot his wife on 16 February, 1941 after a long quarrel in their home. Baraniuk then shot himself. This event was witnessed by Nicholas Marchuk who was a boarder in the house.[111]

The Workers Benevolent Association was allowed to continue its activities and formed a Dramatic Society. Every Sunday evening there were social and cultural activities in their rented hall at 584-3rd Avenue.[112]

In contrast to the left-wing Ukrainians, the local branch of the UNF publicly demonstrated their support for the Canadian war effort. They participated in a parade that included women and children on 7 June, 1941 with a sign that they supported the war effort of the British Empire – Onward for Complete British Victory.

The Quebec Provincial Police, however, arrested Steve Serdar on 18 June, 1941 on a charge of 'making statements intended or likely to cause disaffection, contrary to Regulation 39 of the Defence of Canada Regulations'. Serdar, a Croatian Canadian and Spanish Civil War veteran, was an Organizer for the Communist Party of Canada and was active among the left-wing groups in the Val-d'Or area for some time.[113]

The German invasion of the Soviet Union in June, 1941 proved to be a great internal crisis to the UNF membership across Canada. John

Lenyk and some of the other UNF members heard on a shortwave radio, the news of the entry of the German Army into Lviv in western Ukraine. Now, the traditional enemy of the UNF, the Soviet Union, was an ally of Canada in the war against Nazi Germany. This new system of international alliances changed the attitude of the Canadian federal government towards the Ukrainian nationalist community in Canada. The Department of External Affairs became apprehensive about nationalist claims for the independence of Ukraine and more sensitive to Soviet objections to these claims and this attitude continued throughout the war.

The invasion of the Soviet Union greatly stimulated the efforts of the local Ukrainian pro-communists and a Ukrainian Committee to Aid the Fatherland was formed to raise funds and provide assistance to the Soviet Union. A delegate from Val-d'Or was at the founding convention of this organization.[114] The first mass meeting was held in the Finnish Hall on 11th Street on 27 July, 1941.[115] This Committee claimed that they sought the assistance of the UNF and Vzaimna Pomich (Mutual Aid)[116] but received no reply.[117] The RCMP report stated that the speakers strongly castigated 'Ukrainian pro-Nazi elements in Canada' and demanded that the Ukrainian National Federation and Hetman organization should be banned forthwith and its leaders should be held in concentration camps. The speakers demanded that the properties of these two organizations should be confiscated and that property of ULFTA should be restored to 'Ukrainian workers and farmers of Canada ...' According to the RCMP report, the speakers '... condemned very much the Ukrainian National Federation much more than Hitler and Germany.'[118] It is obvious that the RCMP began to use informants from the left-wing Ukrainian community to obtain their information that could only be provided by participants at these meetings and events.

The annual cycle of cultural and social activities by the pro-communist community was revived but with the intention of aiding the Soviet Union. Their Val-d'Or branch raised $2418.00 for the Red Cross, Perron raised $646.17 and Malartic raised $570.00.[119] Members wrote to the federal government in Ottawa requesting the return of the ULFTA halls across Canada and their property in Val-d'Or. At least three members of the WBA from Val-d'Or[120] and one member from Malartic joined the Canadian Army.[121]

Later, the Ukrainian Committee to Aid the Fatherland was able to rent J. Kolomeychuk's hall which was shared with the local branch of the Federation of Russian Canadians, established in 1942. Almost every evening, social gatherings were held in the hall. The Committee made a determined effort to increase their membership. Appeals were also made to add subscribers to their various newspapers, *Ukrainian Life, Voice of Truth* and *The Canadian Tribune*. According to the RCMP report, the aim of all these newspapers was the same – 'communist revolution.'[122]

Although all the East European groups were invited to participate in their fund-raising activities for the Soviet war effort, the Slovak and Polish groups refused to attend.[123] The RCMP reported that the 'Red elements' in Val-d'Or were receiving some opposition from the '... loyal groups who prefer to support an allied victory directly.'[124] The Polish group was opposed to the Committee that they claimed was spreading communist propaganda rather than concentrating their efforts on helping the war effort.[125] In November, 1941, the Committee to Aid the Fatherland had approximately 50 members in Val-d'Or and were able to attract up to 200 people to their fund-raising events from the local Slavic community.[126] The Committee also held tag-days, banquets and dances to raise funds. On 31 December, 1941, one member of the pro-communist community from Val-d'Or sent a small sum of money and a package of socks and cigarettes to Peter Prokopchak, who was interned in the Hull Jail with the other leaders of the CPC and ULFTA.[127]

In December, 1941, plans were made to establish an evening school for the children. A banquet was held and funds were raised. The school was held on Saturday mornings when music lessons were held between 10:00 and 12:00 a.m. The school was also held Monday, Tuesday, Thursday and Saturday. Reading and writing were taught along with lectures and a fee of $1.00 per child was charged.[128]

The Japanese attack on Pearl Harbor in the Hawaiian Islands on 7 December, 1941, changed the direction of the Second World War with the entry of the United States on the side of Canada and the Allies. The

United States greatly increased their production of war materials and orders flowed into Canada further boosting the Canadian war industry. The orders for war material from the United States stimulated the Canadian war economy and had repercussions in all parts of Canada including Val-d'Or. Also, the large enrolments into the Canadian Armed Forces ensured that unemployment was eliminated in 1942 for all practical purposes and anyone who wanted to work could find employment.

During the summer of 1942, a local branch of the Association of Ukrainian Canadians (AUC) was organized by members of the banned ULFTA and became very active. The local AUC branch worked closely with the Committee to Aid the Fatherland and a number of social events were organized to raise funds for the Soviet war effort. Picnics were held at Blouin Lake almost every weekend. At their rented hall, at the Chateau Inn, and at the lake, there were dances, lunches, discussions and speeches. This method of fundraising continued throughout the war. Enlistment in the Canadian armed forces was encouraged and funds were raised for various Canadian and Soviet war charities. The Federation of Russian Canadians also held fund-raising events and in 1942 collected $6628.00 for the Russian Relief Fund.[129] Between 70 and 200 people regularly attended these events.[130] There were rumours in the local Ukrainian nationalist community that the money raised for the war charities were used to finance communist political activities.[131]

In September, 1942, a representative of the Department of National War Services from Ottawa visited Val-d'Or to investigate the different war charity collections. The RCMP reports noted that local activists travelled to the smaller mining communities such as Perron and Malartic to raise funds for their charities. After some investigation, the RCMP reports concluded that the money raised was forwarded directly to Relief of Russian Refugees Committee.[132] Community and social events were held almost every week during the winter of 1942-43 to raise funds for the Ukrainian pro-communist press and for ambulances and other assistance to the Soviet Union.[133]

The political activities of the Association of Ukrainian Canadians were limited to campaigning for the opening of a Second Front in western

Europe to relieve the German military pressure on the Soviet Union. Locally, the campaign against the Ukrainian nationalist organizations and newspapers continued.[134] On 18 April, 1943, a local ULFTA Defence Committee was established and a meeting was held at the Chateau Inn to gather signatures for a petition to the Canadian federal government to return the confiscated ULFTA property. About 110 persons attended this meeting.[135] A petition was sent to the Chairman of the Defence of Canada Regulations Committee at the Parliament Buildings in Ottawa requesting the lifting of the ban on the ULFTA. The Chairman of the Committee forwarding the petition was T.A. Myslanka and the Secretary was J. Kolisnyk.[136]

On 2 May, 1943, a May Day banquet was held at the rented hall and approximately 130 people attended including local Russians and Croatians. During the year, the left-wing organizations continued to hold social and community events for fund-raising purposes. Funds were also raised for the Kyiv Hospital Fund and the newspaper, *Canadian Tribune*. During July and August, picnics were held at the public beach at Blouin Lake. The events were attended from 70 to 200 people. All these events were regularly reported to the local RCMP by informants.[137] In October, 1943, the local members were particularly elated when the ban on the ULFTA was lifted by the federal government and their organization was again legal.[138]

In December, 1943, the Ukrainian Canadian Association organized another series of lessons for their children. This school was held in their rented hall on 3rd Avenue during the evenings from 5:00 to 8:00 p.m. There were 27 children attending and Ukrainian reading, writing, History of the Soviet Union, political knowledge, music and singing were taught. The teacher came from Leamington, Ontario, and was one of the first graduates of the special schools established by the ULFTA for their teachers and leadership cadres. During the winter, concerts and other social events were regularly held to raise funds for this school.[139]

On 13 February, 1944, the Dramatic Committee gave a presentation of a four-act play based on conditions in Czarist Russia. The RCMP informant was requested to provide more information on the contents of this play. The report concluded that '... The leaders are always using such plays to stimulate hatred among their members and sympathizers towards the rich and the government they do not like.'[140]

The regular series of concerts, banquets and social events continued as opportunities for fund-raising for hospitals in Soviet Ukraine, the children's school, and the press. Picnics were held at the beach at Blouin Lake and dances were held at their rented hall on 3rd Avenue. On 11 June, 1944, the Ukrainian Canadian Association, the Workers Benevolent Association and the ULFTA held a large banquet at the Chateau Inn Grill to celebrate the liberation of Soviet Ukraine from the occupying Nazi German military. Speeches were made praising the Red Army and the Soviet leader, Joseph Stalin. About 100 persons attended this event and $600.00 was collected.[141] Fund-raising continued throughout the summer for various causes. But at least on one occasion, the RCMP report noted that it became evident that their members and sympathizers '... appeared to show very little enthusiasm towards the collection'.[142]

In the provincial elections, members and sympathizers were encouraged to support the Liberal Party as there were no Labor Progressive Party[143] candidates in Abitibi. At a picnic held on 23 July, the speaker said, '... If the working class of the Province of Quebec fail to elect a Liberal government, the reactionaries of the Bloc Populaire and l'Union Nationale will again invoke the padlock-law against progressive and democratic working people of this Province'.[144] The left-wing organizations also canvassed for funds for Labor Progressive Party candidates in Alberta. The speakers explained that '... the French Canadian Population in Quebec required much more education in the class struggle and for this reason all assistance possible should be given to the LPP candidates as they were more likely to be elected in that province [Alberta].'[145]

The Ukrainian left-wing organizations resumed their children's school for the winter season and the activities of this school continued to be monitored by the RCMP. In one report, it was noted that the textbook for the teaching of Soviet history was written by [Soviet] Russian authors.[146]

On Christmas Day, 25 December, 1944, the various left-wing associations held a public dance to raise funds to purchase seeds for the Soviet

Union. Approximately 100 persons were present but, according to the RCMP report, the speaker '... had to refrain from addressing the audience due to many interruptions coming from those who had partaken of alcoholic beverages.'[147]

During the winter months of the new year, 1945, the left-wing associations continued to hold social and cultural events to raise funds for the Soviet Union or for the local children's school. Some of the charities included seeds and clothes for the Soviet Union. After the defeat of the German Army in Stalingrad, the Red Army began to advance westward and liberated large areas of Ukraine. On 25 January, 1945, a concert was held to commemorate the unification of all provinces in Ukraine into one Soviet Ukrainian country. The speaker praised the Soviet leader, Joseph Stalin for liberating all of Ukraine and expressed contempt for Ukrainian nationalists both in Ukraine and in Canada.[148] At these events, there were regularly between 60 and 100 persons present. The Soviet contribution to the eventual defeat of Nazi Germany in 1944-1945 greatly boosted the morale among the left-wing movement across Canada and in Val-d'Or.

As the Second World War progressed, the war industries continued to expand and several Ukrainians left Val-d'Or for southern Ontario and other parts of Canada. There were also departures from the other ethno-cultural groups. Many Finns who had carpentry skills, moved to southern Ontario to work building military barracks and other buildings. The move to other industrial centers may have been encouraged by rumours and the fear that the gold mines might be closed after all gold mining was suspended in the United States.[149] In the years from 1941 until the end of the war in 1945, there were few if any new workers arriving in Val-d'Or. The population stabilized and gradually began to decrease.

In 1943, an all-weather road was built connecting Val-d'Or with Montreal and Ottawa which greatly facilitated travel and communications. Individual Ukrainian workers from the Abitibi area also helped to build this road.

From an examination of the minutes of the local branch of the Ukrainian National Federation, it is readily apparent that few individuals were doing most of the work in the branch. There were no new members and older members were leaving for other parts of Canada or opted for less strenuous work in the branch.[150] On 6 April, 1943, there was an attempt to re-establish a branch of the Ukrainian National Youth Federation of Canada (MUN) with 21 members.[151] At the annual UNF branch meeting held on 2 January, 1944, there were 24 members. At that time, the Youth Branch (MUN) was dissolved and amalgamated with the UNF due to the lack of younger members. The UNF raised funds for the Canadian Red Cross, for children in England and encouraged their members to join the Canadian Reserve Army. The UNF had a large map of Europe on a wall in their hall that they used to discuss the progress of the war and the fate of Ukraine. This map remained on the wall until the 1960s.

In February, 1944, organizers from the pro-Communist Mine, Mill and Smelter Workers Union were sent from Ontario to Val-d'Or to organize the miners. Approximately 90% of the miners supported the Mine Mill Union and the union was certified on 30 June, 1944 at the Golden Manitou Mine and on 25 July, 1944 at the Lamaque Mine.[152]

Among those from the east European communities that enlisted from the region, there were a number of fatal casualties. Alexander Ganjolouski from Val-d'Or was killed in action in Italy on 6 October, 1943. He was a member of the Seaforth Highlanders of Canada. Also in Italy, Peter Shynkarchuk from Pascalis was killed in action on the night of 25/26 March, 1944. He was a member of the 48 Highlanders of Canada. Joseph Peter Chomyshyn from Malartic and a member of the 1st Battalion, Royal Highland Regiment of Canada (Black Watch) was killed in action on 25 July, 1944 in France.[153] His name was the only Ukrainian name included on the local Cenotaph (War Memorial) to the volunteers from Val-d'Or that were fatal casualties during the Second World War.

In England, Ukrainian Canadian soldiers on leave gathered from time to time for social occasions and one of the first social gatherings were held at the Ukrainian Social Club in Manchester where a small Ukrainian community had existed since the First World War. These social gatherings developed into the Ukrainian Canadian Servicemen's Association (UCSA) which was formally constituted in Manchester on 7 January,

1943. Among the charter members was Dmytro Fedorkow from Perron.[154] Fedorkow had served in the Ukrainian National Army in Ukraine as a teenager, then in the Polish Army before immigrating to Canada and at the age of 39, joined the Canadian Army at the outbreak of the Second World War. He is buried in the Protestant cemetery in Val-d'Or.

Another volunteer, Peter Paul Brosko had joined the Royal Canadian Air Force in 1942. His plane was shot down over Oberseebach, Alsace on 29 July, 1944 and he was able to parachute safely to the ground. He was arrested by a German Gendarme and driven in his car but en route, the Gendarme took Brosko out of his car and shot him. His body was thrown into a ditch. This crime was committed in front of witnesses and the Gendarme was later tried for this war crime.[155] Bohdan (Mike) Koshilka, still a teenager, left for the Pacific Coast, joined the Merchant Marine and worked on a ship that made regular crossings of the Pacific Ocean during the war against Japan.[156]

**VE Day in Val-d'Or**, 8 May, 1945.
*Photo credit:* La Société d'histoire et de généalogie de Val-d'Or

On 8 May, VE (Victory in Europe) Day, a large parade was organized in Val-d'Or and the pro-communist organizations took an active part in this event. The parade started at 1:30 p.m. and was led by the town fire trucks, Boy Scouts and a military band. The Federation of Russian Canadians was represented by 60 members, the pro-communist Ukrainian organizations had 80 members and there were 30 Slovenes. There were also Croatian marchers in this parade. Altogether there were approximately 250 marchers.

**VE Day in Val-d'Or**, 8 May, 1945 with Soviet and pro-Tito Yugoslav flags.
*Photo credit:* La Société d'histoire et de généalogie de Val-d'Or

The RCMP informant reported that the marchers carried red flags and a portrait of Marshal Joseph Tito, the new Communist leader of Yugoslavia. The pro-communist organizations unfurled a huge Soviet flag to march in the parade.[157] The pro-Tito Yugoslavs carried a Yugoslav flag with a red star. The members of the local branch of the Ukrainian National Federation refused to march with the communists and chose instead to march with the Bloc Populaire (French Canadian nationalists) group.[158] The RCMP was particularly interested in the display of the Soviet flag and requested more detailed information from their informants. The RCMP informant originally stated there were no British or Canadian flags displayed by the pro-communist marchers however, it was later clarified that there were some small British flags displayed by the Slovenian marchers.[159] This parade was perhaps the peak of their public activities during their existence in Val-d'Or.

During the summer of 1945, the left-wing organizations renewed their series of picnics at Blouin Lake and their social and cultural events at their hall. A delegation from the local branch of the ULFTA was sent to Toronto to attend a two-day national festival in June.[160]

The contributions of the Soviet Union to the final Allied victory and the successful conclusion of the Second World War greatly boosted the morale and prestige of the left-wing organizations in Val-d'Or. In their confidence, a number of organizations wrote a letter on 2 September, 1945 to the Mayor and Town Council of Val-d'Or condemning the local branch of the Ukrainian National Federation. The authors of the letter claimed to represent the Canadian Ukrainian Association, the Canadian Russian Federation, the Canadian Croatian Federation, the Czecho-Slovak Anti-Fascist Organization and the Workers Benevolent Association. They particularly condemned the use of the Ukrainian nationalist blue and yellow flag in parades and in the UNF hall and requested that '... the use of the flag should be forbidden by the Authorities'.[161]

However, the left-wing organizations received a minor setback when the Ukrainian Canadian Association was requested to vacate their rented hall by the end of September. The tenants living over the hall had complained about the levels of noise made when meetings were held.

The association then moved their activities to the Finnish Hall on 11<sup>th</sup> Street. A committee was formed to investigate the possibility of building their own hall.[162]

The RCMP continued to monitor the local activities of the left-wing organizations. The RCMP reported on one meeting held on 30 September, 1945 where the speaker remarked that the ULFTA schools had produced thousands of students who were now '... able leaders in workers movements throughout the Dominion'. The RCMP report concluded that '... This is an open acknowledgement that the schools do propagate Communistic doctrines sufficiently completely to make potential leaders in subversive activities.'[163]

Second World War Cenotaph in Val-d'Or with names of the local casualties
*Photo credit:* Myron Momryk

# THE DISPLACED PERSONS: THE THIRD WAVE OF UKRAINIAN IMMIGRATION

## 1946-1952

With the end of the Second World War, the left-wing organizations renewed their open hostility towards the local Ukrainian nationalists. In February, 1946, a notice was circulated among the members of the Ukrainian left-wing organizations that '... Any member of the Association be found to be a subscriber to any of the aforementioned papers (*Ukrainian Voice, New Pathway, Canadian Farmer, Ukrainian News*), that member would be expelled from the Association.'[164] Among the resolutions from the annual convention was the report of a campaign to convert as many Ukrainian nationalists to their cause. This was part of a larger campaign to prevent the Ukrainian nationalists in Canada from collecting large sums of money to assist Ukrainian refugees and Displaced Persons in western Europe and also to prevent them from spreading unfavourable 'propaganda' against the Soviet Union.[165]

A radio program was sponsored by the left-wing organizations on the local radio station CKVD on Sunday morning, 14 April, 1946. The radio program consisted of musical renditions and announcements.[166] The left-wing organizations continued their annual series of social events began during the Second World War including picnics at Blouin Lake during the summer. These events were opportunities to raise funds for various causes including the training of new teachers and supporting local left-wing political candidates.[167] Between 65 and 100 persons regularly attended these events. In 1946, the local pro-communist Yugoslav community in Val-d'Or raised $1233.55 and in Malartic $134.00 was raised for a national total of $10,645.55 for X-Ray equipment in Yugoslavia.[168] The local branch of the Federation of Russian Canadians raised funds for their newspaper, *Vestnik* and to build the Russian People's Hall in Vancouver and in Montreal. On 20 November, 1947 a Russian Concert was held at the Marocco Club with artists from Toronto and over 300 persons attended. In 1949, the FRC had 23 members and the Workers Benevolent Association had 21 members. Their library had 200 books.[169]

On 17 November, 1946, the local left-wing organizations under the auspices of the Joint Slav Committee, celebrated the 29th anniversary of the Russian Revolution at the Finnish Hall. There were 127 persons present and the RCMP informant noted that the speakers praised the Soviet Union and the Soviet leader, Joseph Stalin.[170] But, already during 1946, the optimism of the immediate post-Second World War period began to fade and the reality of the Cold War began to intrude into the daily life of Canadians. The defection of Igor Gouzenko, a cypher clerk, from the Soviet Legation in Ottawa in late 1945 with evidence of Soviet spying in Canada contributed to the growing Cold War atmosphere. Among the Ukrainian community in Val-d'Or, the Cold War continued and the tensions between the pro-communists and the nationalists escalated.

With the end of the war in Europe, UNF members were encouraged to assist Ukrainian refugees and Displaced Persons[171] stranded in Displaced Persons Camps in western Europe. These Ukrainian refugees had refused to return to a Soviet-dominated Ukraine. Although the Second World War ended in western Europe in May, 1945, a guerilla war by the Ukrainian Insurgent Army against the Soviet administration in western Ukraine and eastern Poland continued until the early 1950s. Severe Soviet repression of the Ukrainian nationalist movement also prevented many Displaced Persons from returning to Ukraine.

Funds were raised across Canada by the Ukrainian Canadian Committee and contacts established with Ukrainians in the various Displaced Persons Camps. There was also interest generated at the local level by members of the European community in helping the Displaced Persons. In June, 1947, Theodore Koulomozine, a prominent member of the local Russian anti-communist community, spoke to the Rotary Club about the problems of the refugees.[172] Those who had relatives among the refugees began proceedings to sponsor and bring them to Canada. Some of the first Ukrainian Displaced Persons and refugees who arrived in Canada were sponsored by their relatives in Val-d'Or. Among the first Ukrainian refugees to arrive in the region was Stanley Klosevych who arrived in Lac Castagnier with his parents. Stanley's parents were given a farm complete with a root cellar full of vegetables. Stanley stayed only for a few weeks before he left for Toronto to continue his education. His parents stayed for a year before they also moved to Toronto.[173]

There were departures from the Ukrainian nationalist community.[174] In 1946, Ivan Lenyk left with his family for Toronto. He was a well-known community leader and one of the founders of the UNF Branch in Val-d'Or.[175] He was also one of the few Ukrainian businessmen. He sold his store next to the UNF Hall to a French Canadian veteran and with his savings, Lenyk was able to enter the Toronto real estate market.

Among those who passed away on April 28, 1947 was Stefan Waskan. He was originally a member of the Ukrainian Social Democratic Party in Canada (USDP) during the First World War and was invited to speak at a political event in Ottawa on 1 May, 1918. This event was raided by the police and he was arrested as a suspected 'Bolshevik'. He was released because he was already naturalized and a British subject. The charge against Stefan Waskan was withdrawn and ordered to leave Ottawa and he left for Toronto.[176] He continued his involvement in Ukrainian socialist politics and with Pavlo Krat, Ivan Stefanitsky and Mykola Yeremiychuk formed a Committee of Aid to Ukrainian Emigrants (CAUE). The USDP did not approve of the committee and this brought on a new struggle in the party.[177] He left the Communist movement in 1923. Waskan eventually made his way to Edmonton and from the fall of 1930 he became a close friend of Antin Hlynka. Waskan wrote two booklets, the English language *Behind the Green Door* about alcoholism, and a Ukrainian Drama, *Danylyshyn and Bilas*. In the City Directory for the City of Edmonton, he is listed in 1935 as an 'author'. In the fall of 1935, he was one of the founders of the newspaper, *Klych (The Call)* with Antin Hlynka and William Dorosh. This was an anti-communist newspaper and sought to promote united action among Ukrainian Canadians. The first issue of *Klych* was published in January, 1935. The Depression obliged Waskan to leave the newspaper and search for work. In 1940, he was working as a bartender in Edmonton. Waskan was a member of UNF in Val-d'Or when he passed away in 1947 and his funeral was arranged by Mr. M. Kruk. He is buried in an unmarked grave in Edmonton. Antin Hlynka was later elected to Parliament in Ottawa. Waskan was one of the few political 'intellectuals' in the UNF at that time.

The continuing stream of workers from the outlying resource industries to the manufacturing centers in the larger cities across Canada greatly reduced the number of miners. The dangerous working conditions at the mines and reports of mine accidents did not encourage an over supply of applicants.[178] In April and May, 1947, an underground mining accident at the East Malartic mine in Malartic left twelve miners killed. This story made the headlines in many major newspapers across Canada. The mine had employed 450 men and 225 of them worked underground. When the surface workers were recalled only a handful came to work while 30 of the underground workers left to work in other mines.[179] In 1948-1950, at least four miners with East European names

**Ukrainian Miners at the Golden Manitou Mine**, June 9, 1949
*From left to right:* John Sikorsky, Paul Zbihlyj, unidentified, Victor Ulanowicz, John Chmyliwsky, recent Displaced Persons. *Photo credit:* Mike Zbihlyj

were killed working in the local mines.[180] At one mine accident, Watsik Koltak, a recent Polish Displaced Person who worked as a miner, saved six other miners but lost his own life.[181]

Among the European community in the Val-d'Or region in 1947-1948, there were individual cases of pro-communists returning to their country of origin mainly to Yugoslavia.[182] These individuals were certainly among the more dedicated supporters of the left-wing movement in the Abitibi area. Their departure, no doubt, weakened this movement at a time when the arrival of the DPs presented a challenge to their political ideology and activities. There were also individual cases from the Ukrainian, Czech, Slovak, Hungarian and Polish communities who left for Europe. However, soon after their arrival in their countries of origin, many returnees especially those from Yugoslavia, requested to return to Canada. The political and economic conditions, the low standards of living and the war damages made their life more difficult than they had expected. In some cases, they experienced open hostility from the local population who greatly suffered during the war and resented the arrival of the well-fed Canadians who did not have to endure these sufferings. Those who had departed for the Soviet Union and then regretted their decision, were rarely given permission to return to Canada.

In January, 1949, the local branches of the AUUC, WBA, and FRC worked together to organize a Peace demonstration but the Croatian Fraternal Union and the Council of Canadian South Slavs were reluctant to participate because of the political split between Marshal Tito of Yugoslavia and the Soviet leader, Joseph Stalin. This political dispute in eastern Europe divided the pro-communist organizations in Val-d'Or into two mutually hostile groups and further weakened the local left-wing movement. In 1949, a local branch of the Canadian Slav Committee was founded to maintain and demonstrate Slav solidarity among the pro-communist organizations and raise funds for various causes.

In general, many of the returning demobilized Canadian soldiers were not interested in the heavy physical work in the mines, farms and forests but sought work in modern factories in the larger industrial centers with social and cultural amenities. Other veterans continued their education or attended trade schools. Also, the pay in the mines in Quebec was not competitive with occupations in other parts of Canada. For example, dishwashers in British Columbia lumber camps earned $7.41 per day compared to $7.26 per day for experienced miners and timbermen.[183] The Canadian federal government feared that the post-war years would be marked by an economic recession similar to the post-First World War period and continued the policy of limiting immigration to Canada. A labour shortage soon developed in the resource sectors of the economy.

The problem of labour shortage dated back to the closing days of the Second World War. In a report from July, 1945, the manpower situation was "… so critical that three mines are faced with shutdown unless they obtain men within two months." Employment was therefore open only to single men and married men who were willing to leave their families behind. This situation was due to the lack of housing in all mining communities. Also there was a large percentage of rejections due to the high physical standards required for work in the mines. The labour turnover in the mines was calculated to be 20% per month as compared to 12% in 1940. At that time, twenty-two producing mines employed 7000 men when they normally employed 10,000 men.[184]

One early solution to this problem was the decision to allow Polish Army veterans to immigrate from England to Canada on contracts to work in agriculture. These Polish veterans had refused to return to Poland dominated by the Soviet Union especially since eastern Poland where many of the soldiers originated, was now incorporated into Soviet Ukraine and Soviet Belorus. News of this federal government decision was met with hostility among the local left-wing organizations. At a banquet sponsored by the pro-Communist Press Fund Committee held on 24 November, 1946, the speakers protested against this action denouncing the Polish veterans as '… Polish fascists from Italy, who … will spread anti-Soviet propaganda in Canada and act as 'Scabs' whenever the Canadian capitalists need them.'[185]

The left-wing organizations maintained their series of social and cultural events through the winter months. Rather than renew the

Ukrainian Labor Farmer Temple Association (ULFTA) that was banned in 1940, former members of the ULFTA founded a new national organization, the Association of United Ukrainian Canadians (AUUC). In 26-31 March, 1947, an organizer from Lachine, Quebec visited Val-d'Or as part of a campaign to increase membership. A Ukrainian Youth Club was established as well as a Women's Branch of the Association of United Ukrainian Canadians.[186]

The end of the Second World War encouraged the prospectors to continue prospecting in northern Quebec and also into the Northwest Territories. John (Jack) Matthews, described in *The Val d'Or Star* as 'one of Canada's best known prospectors' visited Val-d'Or in September, 1947 on his way to Chibougamau, a new mining centre north-east of Val-d'Or. He had earlier worked in the Yellowknife area where he made a gold discovery and staked his first claim in May, 1945. The Tundra Mine, founded by Matthews, eventually began production in 1964 but soon closed down due to its isolation and heavy air transportation costs of mining material.[187] Another Ukrainian prospector/developer was John Manchulenko who became one of the stakers of Marchant Mining in Abitibi in the mid-1950s.[188] Unfortunately some individual prospectors became enmeshed in legal issues. Frank Gryciuk, a 'Ukraine-born prospector' also known as 'Souzy' was charged with perjury in alleged illegal transactions of gold and his story appeared *The Val d'Or Star* in December, 1953.[189]

The mining companies faced constant turnovers in their staff and petitioned the federal government for miners or else they threatened to shut down operations due to lack of labour.[190] In the years 1945-47, the Canadian government was also petitioned by Ukrainian, Polish and other ethnocultural groups to allow the entry of the European refugees in the Displaced Persons Camps in Germany. By 1947, the Canadian government resolved to deal with these two problems at once. They agreed to allow the refugees in through various 'bulk labour schemes' on condition that the new immigrants worked one-year contracts in mining, lumbering or agriculture.[191] The ship passage of the miners would be pre-paid from Germany. Val-d'Or was among the first communities to receive these Displaced Persons. The new miners, Ukrainians, Poles, Lithuanians, Latvians and others were also sent to Malartic, Perron, Duparquet, Cadillac and other mine sites.

The fixed price of gold set by the United States at $35.00 an ounce in the early 1930s did not reflect the growing costs of mine production. This fixed price obliged the Canadian federal government to pass the Emergency Gold Mining Assistance Act in 1948 that relieved the general mining situation although on a temporary basis.[192]

The mining companies sent recruiting committees to the Displaced Persons Camps in Germany and selected potential miners from the applicant refugees.[193] Members of the selection team were W.H. Wright of the Canadian Metal Mining Association, Georges Schmelzl, formerly of Sigma Mines and John Kostuik, Mine Superintendent at Sladen Malartic Mines, who spoke Polish.[194] According to some reports in the local press, approximately 2,000 DP miners could be expected. The initial requests in October, 1947 were as follows: Cadillac-Malartic - 75 miners, Lamaque/Siscoe - 150 miners and Noranda - 69 miners.[195]

Main Street, Val-d'Or, at the time of the arrival of the Ukrainian Displaced Persons to Val-d'Or.
*Photo credit:* La Société d'histoire et de généalogie de Val-d'Or

In addition to screening for physical fitness, the miner applicants were also screened for their political views. Robert Haddow, a union official and member of the Labor Progressive Party, inquired about an appointment to the recruiting committee to travel to Europe to select fur workers in the Displaced Persons Camps. On 4 June, 1948, Robert MacNamara, a federal government official, replied to Robert Haddow that '... You can take it as a fact that no one will be sent overseas to select displaced persons if he is a Communist. One of the duties is to ensure that displaced persons selected for admission to Canada are not Communist and obviously it is my duty not to recommend a man who is himself a Communist.'[196]

The contract workers came to Val-d'Or during the first few months of 1948. They were selected for their physical abilities and stamina. Almost all were under the age of thirty years and most lived in bunkhouses provided by the mining companies. Because of the shortage of miners, they were sent to work within a few days of their arrival. Since the shortage of housing continued to be a problem in Val-d'Or, those miners with families had to leave their wives and children behind in Displaced Persons Camps in Germany until suitable accommodations could be found in Val-d'Or.[197] The new miners were required to present a document certifying that they were able to rent an apartment or rooms before their families were given permission to arrive from Germany. It was only six months or later that the wives began to arrive with their children.

The wives and children crossed the Atlantic Ocean in the same ships that were used earlier to transport the returning Canadian soldiers from Europe. They landed in Halifax or Quebec City and then began to long train ride across northern Quebec to Val-d'Or where they were met by their waiting husbands and fathers. In some cases, their first view of Val-d'Or was a disappointment because they had lived and worked in German urban centres with more impressive stone and brick buildings with paved streets rather than the tar-paper covered wooden structures with unpaved roads.

Because most of the new immigrants came from eastern Europe with Polish or German identification documents, their names were spelled according to these alphabets and many kept the Polish or German spellings throughout their lives in Canada. A few of the new immigrants deliberately withheld information about their higher education so that they could be admitted to Canada as miners. In one case, Alexander Peter Lapko, a Ukrainian medical doctor originally from the Donbas region of Soviet Ukraine, was able to pass the interview and was accepted as a miner. But after two weeks in the Lamaque mine, management discovered his qualifications. He then requested an early release from his contract and the doctor left for Toronto where he eventually reentered the medical profession.[198] Others with higher education stayed and completed their contracts.

In almost all cases, the new miners arrived on one day and the next day they were already working. The fact that the miners were guaranteed employment and were earning wages greatly increased their morale and their positive attitude towards their new circumstances. For most Ukrainians who arrived at that time, their work as miners was the first regular civilian employment since the outbreak of the Second World War in September, 1939.

The arrival of the immigrant workers in Val-d'Or from the Displaced Persons Camps had an immediate effect on the ethnocultural community. A few Polish DPs attended a dance held on 29 February, 1948 in the Finnish Hall by the left-wing organizations. A fight broke out when the Poles were called 'fascists' by one of the local members. Attempts by some of the local left-wingers to persuade the new immigrants to join the CIO labour union were not successful.[199]

The new Ukrainian immigrants were warmly greeted by the Ukrainian nationalist community in Val-d'Or. Many of the immigrant miners visited the UNF Hall. On 14 March, 1948, there were 33 persons at a meeting of which 14 applied for membership in the UNF. On 12 December, 1948, there were 56 members in the UNF Branch. In April 1949, there were 16 new subscribers to the newspaper, *Novyi Shliakh* (The New Pathway).[200] The new immigrants participated in the various cultural events at the UNF hall. No known DPs joined the Ukrainian pro-communist organizations.[201]

The UNF branch continued to send funds for various projects in other parts of Canada and contributed to the building of the UNF hall in Toronto.[202] The UNF branch had formed a Ridna Shkola (School) Committee to administer the Ukrainian School. The children would also recite poetry and sing in their choir at the various concerts and other events. However, the school was interrupted when the teacher soon left for Toronto.[203]

Religious services had been provided since 1940 by visiting Ukrainian Catholic clergy from eastern Ontario.[204] There were also occasional visits by Ukrainian Orthodox clergy. In 1948-49, religious services were provided by Father Michael Horoshko, a Ukrainian Catholic priest, who visited Val-d'Or by car from Kirkland Lake. During his visits, he would hold religious services in the Roman Catholic Church or the UNF Hall. Father Horoshko, a former chaplain in the Canadian Army during the Second World War, also campaigned against the local communists among the Ukrainian community.[205]

**Anti-Communist parade in Val-d'Or**, 2 May, 1948 with Wasyl Poremski leading the UNF group.
*Photo credit:* Al Hnatiuk

The recent Ukrainian immigrants were all strongly anti-communist and were vocal in denouncing the Soviet Union. The local Knights of Columbus chapter sponsored an anti-communist rally where the main speaker was a former Soviet officer who escaped in 1944. Over 100 recent immigrants attended this meeting.[206] There were rumours that there were approximately 3,000 pro-Communists in Abitibi and that a clandestine communist radio station had been operating in the Val-d'Or area.[207] Among other rumours, the pro-Communist organizations were planning a large demonstration on May Day, 1948. One local organization that was identified as pro-Communist was the League of Croatian Canadians. To counter this manifestation, a Val d'Or Anti-Communist Committee was formed and conducted an anti-communist and pro-democracy campaign in Val-d'Or for one month.[208] A large parade was organized on 2 May, 1948 with over a thousand participants that included the Knights of Columbus, marching band, school children, members from various communities – Poles, Lithuanians, Finns, and also French Canadians and English Canadians. The Lithuanians sang as they marched. The UNF took part of this parade with Wasyl Poremsky leading the UNF group. He was followed by flag-bearers and UNF members including women and children. They also carried the Union Jack. Speeches were made by Rev. Father Titus Wiktor, the Polish Catholic priest, denouncing Communism.[209] According to *The Globe and Mail*, the *Toronto Daily Star* and a RCMP report, one of the largest anti-Communist parades in Canada was held in Val-d'Or at this time.[210] Vehicles with anti-Communist slogans and banners were also took part in this parade. Despite the local rumours, the pro-Communists made no public demonstrations.

When Vasyl Terecio from the National Executive of the AUUC, visited Val d'Or on 9 April, 1948, some of the new Ukrainian immigrants attended this meeting and disputed his statements on events in the Soviet Union. This confrontation created some confusion among the local members of the AUUC. The new immigrants were denounced as 'fascists'.[211]

At the local level, contacts between the UNF members and the Ukrainian communists were forbidden. In 1948, for example, one member of the UNF executive had to resign for publicly socializing with the local communists. However, some of local pro-communists had the opportunity to discuss political events in Ukraine with the new miners while working underground. For some, it was the first opportunity to discuss the Stalinist abuses of the 1930s and the Second World War in Ukraine with eyewitnesses. The arrival of the DPs was seen as a threat by the pro-communist groups. They also complained to their headquarters in Toronto and Winnipeg about their isolation from the larger centers and that organizers did not visit them frequently or at all.[212]

The newly arrived Displaced Persons were condemned by some of the active local Ukrainian communists and their press as 'war criminals' and traitors for refusing to return to Soviet Ukraine and help rebuild the country devastated by the war.[213] The Displaced Persons were, however, defended by the local mine management.[214] On 5 December, 1948, an AUUC meeting was held in the Finnish Hall to hear a speaker from Toronto. About 35 AUUC members were present including about 20 new Ukrainian immigrants. Before the meeting started, the new immigrants were told that the meeting was private and that they should leave. When the immigrants refused to leave, the local police were called and the DPs left under protest. The DPs gathered at the UNF Hall and after some discussion, thirty-five men returned to the Finnish Hall later in the afternoon with the intention of chasing the speaker out of town. Although the doors were unlocked and the lights were on, the Hall was empty. The DPs organized themselves into groups of five or six and began to visit the private homes of known AUUC members in their search for the speaker. They monitored the homes for some time but could not locate the speaker.[215]

Dances and other social activities by the left-wing organizations continued but no publicity was made to advertise these activities and all members were notified verbally. Approximately 100 persons attended these activities including two recent immigrants who were generally despised by the other DP immigrants.[216]

The agitation against the new immigrants continued. In April, 1949, a new Ukrainian immigrant working at the Sullivan Mines persuaded the local communists that he was sympathetic to their concerns and would speak on conditions in the Soviet Union. A meeting was called by the local branch of the AUUC and the Federation of Russian Canadians on a Sunday afternoon under the chairmanship of George Zapototsky in the Finnish Hall. Before an audience of approximately 100 persons, the Ukrainian immigrant told the crowd that they had no idea what hell existed behind the Iron Curtain and denounced the Soviet Union. He was booed from the stage and escorted from the hall.[217]

Few public meetings and events were held by the Ukrainian left-wing community in Val-d'Or during the summer months because the poor ventilation and the heat in the Finnish Hall made events too uncomfortable. More frequently, their meetings and celebrations were held in small groups in private homes.[218]

The Ukrainian Displaced Persons were also received by the local French Canadian community with less than an enthusiastic welcome. Opposition to the DP immigration and labour movement was more vocal in Quebec than in other parts of Canada. One of the spokesmen of this opposition was Real Caouette, M.P., who represented the northwestern Quebec constituency of Pontiac in the House of Commons. On 10 March, 1949, Real Caouette spoke on the question of the new DP miners in his area.

> 'I am not against DPs nor against immigrants. They probably are perfect gentlemen, good Catholics and I have met many of them. I must protest energetically and vehemently against the government allowing mining companies in Abitibi and the northwestern part of the province to instigate such irrational immigration which only serves to cause anxiety in our Canadian families in the district. We have unemployed men in Val d'Or, Malartic, Rouyn, Noranda and Duparquet. We have unemployed men in all cities of the district.'[219]

Real Caouette explained why he was opposed to the DP miners but also gave his interpretation for the preference for immigrant labour.

'Mr. Beauchemin (the owner of East Sullivan Mines Ltd.) recently admitted to me, during a conversation we had on the train, that French Canadians were not suited for mining work and that it was necessary to bring displaced persons from Europe for underground work in the mines. The mining companies that have applied for DP labour are letting our own people go without work.'[220]

The Department of Labour was seriously concerned about these accusations and launched an investigation to study the situation. A report was produced which explained the high turnover and lack of experienced miners in the Abitibi area. The report stated that

'... 1948 was a year of marked improvement in the mining industry. This was due to three principal factors: (1) High prices for base metals (2) Dominion Government cost-aid to gold mines and (3) Much improved conditions of steady labour owing to the procurement of displaced persons.

Without the services of substantial numbers of displaced persons and the other factors mentioned above many mines in the Abitibi area and elsewhere would have been compelled to cease operations. The effect of the introduction of displaced persons has been to increase mining activities and so to increase employment opportunities for Canadians, as well as to sustain the general commercial activities of the towns which depend on the mines.'[221]

In January, 1949, the first group of forty Lithuanian miners gave their thanks in a public ceremony upon the completion of their contracts. They had arrived in Val-d'Or on 13 February, 1948.[222] Most left for the larger industrial centers in southern Ontario. Many Ukrainian miners also left on completion of their contracts. More miners were recruited from the Displaced Persons Camps in Germany. During the years, 1947-1952, 6,179 miners arrived as immigrants in Canada.[223]

| Years | Number |
|---|---|
| 1947-1948 | 1,003 |
| 1948-1949 | 1,964 |
| 1949-1950 | 957 |
| 1950-1951 | 649 |
| 1951-1952 | 1,666 |
| 1952-1953 | (none) |

Many of these miner-immigrants worked in the Val-d'Or area. However, there continued to be a larger number of males compared to females in the Ukrainian community and this situation persisted for many years.

Some Ukrainian miners were intent on earning as much as possible to establish themselves and competed for the better-paid jobs in the mines which were often the most dangerous. One brawl over work assignments resulted in a court case and a jail term of two months for a newly-arrived Ukrainian miner because he was '... not yet accustomed to Canadian customs'.[224] There was one case of a recently-arrived Ukrainian miner losing his arm in a mine accident but he remained in Val d'Or and continued to work at the mine.[225] Not all Ukrainian miners were satisfied with their employment in the mines. For example, at the Pickle Crow mine in northern Ontario, twenty Ukrainians who had come to Canada on forestry contracts refused to work at the gold mine creating some concern at the Department of Labour in Ottawa.[226]

The new immigrants also had some difficulties with other 'Canadian customs'. As in most mining towns, there was a tradition established by the local police to raid certain hotels and public buildings for violations of liquor and other laws. On 26 June, 1949, the local branch of the Polish Mutual Aid Society held a dance which was raided by the local police and 174 people were charged as 'found ins'. However, the $10,000 in bail was returned when the charge of serving liquor without a license was dropped due to lack of evidence.[227] This incident soured relations between the European immigrants and the local police authorities for some time.

The local authorities were also not very receptive to the outdoor preaching by Rev. Lorne T. Heron, a new minister of the local Baptist

Church. Rev. Heron and his followers were preaching on various street corners in downtown Val-d'Or on several occasions in 1949 and, as a result, were arrested and sentenced to terms in the Amos Jail. It seems that the real reason for preventing street meetings was mentioned by Mayor Oza Tetrault who stated, "If we give them permission to hold street meetings, how can we stop Communist gatherings?"[228] Reports of these incidents were brought to the attention of Louis St. Laurent, the Minister of Justice in Ottawa. These reports were published in various Canadian national newspapers and also the New York Herald Tribune in the United States.[229]

An Easter Divine Liturgy followed by a banquet was held at the UNF Hall in April, 1950. Fr. S. Shavel was the visiting clergy. Managers of the local mines were invited as well as a local doctor and a French Canadian politician. Herman Sawiuk as President of the UNF Branch made a speech promoting tolerance and unity in the community. The program included songs and dances by the children of UNF members taught by Miss Evdokia Stasiuk.[230]

Despite the local objections of some French Canadian organizations and other difficulties, the DP 'bulk labour schemes' continued and it was through these programs that most of the 32,000 Ukrainian DPs and refugees with their families entered Canada between 1948 and 1952. It was from this group that the Ukrainian DPs came to Val-d'Or after the Second World War.

# BUILDING THE COMMUNITY

## 1950-1954

During the years after the Second World War, Val-d'Or developed from a mining village to a modern town with most of the municipal services although the town still retained many of the characteristics of a mining camp.²³¹ In 1948, the town had a population of 8,000 and was a commercial and regional center for a population of 25,000 people living in a radius of 45 km. Although the town had twelve hotels, the housing problem continued to be a primary concern for miners and their families for several more years. New houses were erected as building material became available. The municipal authorities expanded the waterworks and sewerage systems, laid new streets and sidewalks and paved the main streets of the town. A modern 100-bed hospital and sports arena with a seating capacity of 5,000 people were built to meet the needs of the growing population.²³² In October, 1949, Percival High School was completed to serve the local English Protestant community. A large percentage of students at this school were from the European immigrant community. An electric fence was constructed around the high school to keep out bears that were known to roam in the neighborhood.²³³

In 1949, a local airport with a 1219 metres paved runway was built and a regular air service was established with Montreal in November, 1949 easing the isolation of Val-d'Or.²³⁴ In 1952, the runway was increased to 1,828 metres and the Department of National Defence assumed the management of the airport in 1954. A large Royal Canadian Air Force military base was established.²³⁵ The base provided employment for many residents of Val-d'Or for several decades.

Gradually the Displaced Persons Camps in Germany were closed as the refugees found new homes in Canada, United States and Australia. By 1951, there were few if any new Ukrainian immigrants arriving to work in the mines. The mining companies began to recruit Germans and Italians in Europe as mine workers.²³⁶

According to the 1951 census, there were 503 Ukrainians in Abitibi County. In Val-d'Or and Bourlamaque, there were 299, Malartic - 71, Duparquet - 32, Cadillac - 12 with 89 in the remainder of the County that included Lac Castagnier and Perron.[237] The population of Val-d'Or was approximately 9,000 people and the French Canadians were 70%, the English Canadians were 8% and the 'Foreigners' were 22% of the population.[238] The number of Ukrainians in Abitibi grew as young couples produced a small 'baby boom' during the years 1950-1956 as documented in the number of Baptisms.[239] The numbers of these new children were added to the children who were born in the Displaced Persons Camps and arrived in Canada with their parents. It should be mentioned that there was a larger 'baby boom' among the other ethnocultural groups and especially among the local Anglophone and French Canadian population. There were enough children born at this time in the Ukrainian community that most spoke Ukrainian at home and among their Ukrainian friends. It was only when the children began to attend the local schools that they began to learn English.

All the Ukrainian Displaced Persons were survivors of the Second World War and many took part in Ukrainian nationalist organizations either in Ukraine or in Germany. Their political philosophy was based on the struggles and events during the Second World War. The older members of the UNF branch however, still remembered the events surrounding the Ukrainian War of Liberation during 1918-1921. They arrived in Canada during the 1920s and lived through the Depression and the Second World War in Canada. During this period, they became 'Canadianized' although they retained their Ukrainian identity. The newer arrivals after the Second World War were more fervent Ukrainian nationalists and very quickly political and personality differences arose between the more vocal new immigrants and the older generation of immigrants. An example was the dispute that arose when the new DP members of the UNF branch began to subscribe to the new newspaper, *Homin Ukrainy* (The Ukrainian Echo), which began publishing in 1949 in Toronto. UNF members were discouraged from reading this newspaper and instead were persuaded to subscribe to *Novyi Shlakh* (The New

Pathway), the official organ of the UNF. Some of the DPs resented this political interference in their reading habits and resigned from the UNF branch. Some of these members then began to organize a local branch of the Ukrainian Youth Association (SUM [CYM] Soiuz Ukrainskoi Molodi). [240]

The Ukrainian Youth Association was established as a youth organization in Germany in 1946 by the Bandera faction of the Organization of Ukrainian Nationalists. Within a few years, the association accepted members as young as six years old to over 30 years old. The association became active in Canada in 1948. The ideological program of this association combined Christianity and Ukrainian nationalism and was militantly anti-Soviet.[241]

The early 1950s were the peak years of the Cold War. The Korean War was in progress and threatened to spread to other parts of the world. The local RCAF base was used to train jet pilots who often overflew the town on their training missions. Two Ukrainian volunteers from Val-d'Or joined the Canadian Army during the Korean War.[242] Bohdan (Bob) Stasyshyn, joined the Royal 22$^{nd}$ Regiment, trained at Fort Lewis, Washington, USA. His parents were active members of the UNF Branch in Val-d'Or. After serving in Korea, Bob Stasyshyn returned to Val-d'Or, married and began a long career in local business and community service. [243]

The Association of United Ukrainian Canadians (AUUC) did not have their own hall but had to use the Finnish Hall for which they paid $2.00 for a meeting and $10.00 for a dance or banquet. During August and September, 1950 the AUUC in cooperation with the local branch of the Federation of Russian Canadians (FRC) purchased the Finnish Hall from the Finnish Organization of Canada (FOC) for an estimated price of $5,500.00. Possession of the hall was made on 15 September, 1950. The official documents were prepared and Tony Myslowka, President and George Zapototsky, Secretary, signed as representatives of AUUC Val-d'Or Branch 21 and Fred Biegal, President and Max Mshar, Secretary, signed on behalf of the local branch of the Federation of Russian Canadians.

According to the RCMP report, plans originally were made to have two trustees from each organization, the AUUC and the FRC, to personally purchase the Finnish Hall. This plan was an attempt to circumvent the Quebec Padlock Law. However, this plan was not executed and according to the act of sale, it was clear that both organizations were the sole and legal owners of the building. The name of the building was changed to the Val d'Or Public Hall and offered for rent to any organization. The official opening of the hall was made with a banquet held on 12 November, 1950. Dances and other social events were held to raise money for the purchase of the hall.[244] Because of the growing hostility of the recently arrived DPs, members of the AUUC increasingly held their social events and meetings in private homes.[245] At these meetings, funds were collected for various causes including the support of the Ukrainian left-wing press in Canada.[246]

On 29 June, 1951, the Quebec Provincial Police raided the homes of the more prominent leaders of the left-wing movement in Val-d'Or under the provisions of the Padlock Law. During these raids the complete organizational records of the local AUUC were seized in a private home. As a result of these raids, public organizational activities effectively ceased. Local members avoided the hall in fear that they may be raided again. The local AUUC leadership adopted a 'wait and see' attitude pending legal appeals.[247]

Ukrainians in Val-d'Or made the news in Toronto when a story appeared in *The Globe and Mail* about Nick Karluchik who killed a mother of six children and then himself. Not much is known about Karluchik. He was born in 1897 in Bukovyna and immigrated to Canada in 1913. He worked in Timmins as a miner and in Val-d'Or, according to some reports, he drove a taxi. It seems that he killed this women over a debt that she allegedly owned him. He then killed himself.[248]

The Cold War also affected issues of labour relations and union activities in the gold mines. In 1953, the United Steelworkers of America called a strike in the gold mines of northern Ontario and northern Quebec. The strike was centered in Timmins, Ontario and in Noranda, Quebec and involved twenty mine properties and approximately ten thousand workers. After several months of unsuccessful negotiations, the United States government became especially interested in this regional strike and sought to encourage the Canadian federal government to intervene and bring the strike to an end. They were afraid that if the strike failed, the Mine, Mill and Smelter Workers Union, a pro-communist union, would gain influence and replace the United Steelworkers of America union in the region.

In a memorandum dated 10 November, 1953, the Labour Attaché at the Canadian Embassy in Washington wrote,

> '... This would provide the Communists with a listening and operating post in the North, at the lower rim of the Northern perimeter where the Governments of both Canada and the United States are currently plotting necessary radar defence facilities. Because of this factor, security consideration has a degree of importance beyond the settlement of wages, working conditions and union security. A reasonably satisfactory settlement on the aforesaid issues would maintain the Steelworkers union in the Gold mining areas and keep the Communist union and its conspiratorial agencies out of the territory.'[249]

Eventually the miners in the Val-d'Or region were represented by the United Steelworkers of America union.

**Ukrainian Youth Association (Soiuz Ukrainskoi Molodi)**
In 1951, a founding committee was formed of four members to establish a branch of the Soiuz Ukrainskoi Molodi (SUM - CYM) in Val-d'Or. This organization supported the more militant Ukrainian nationalist and anti-communist political philosophy identified with the leadership of Stefan Bandera.[250] The first meeting was held on 16 March, 1952 and 26 persons joined the new organization named after Bohdan Khmelnitsky, the legendary Ukrainian Cossack leader. Also, the first executive of eight persons was elected.[251] The early meetings were held in private homes, rented facilities and in one case, in the clubrooms of the local

French Canadian Boy Scouts. Most of the new SUM members were former members of the UNF branch. With individual members completing their contracts and moving to the industrial centers and also because of the formation of the new SUM branch, membership in the local UNF branch fell to 25-34 members. After 1952, it was never more than 20 members.[252]

The first meeting of the SUM branch took place on 1 August, 1952. There were 37 members including 8 women. During the first year, the SUM branch held 14 executive meetings and 12 general meetings. In 1953-1954, there were 37 members but with the departure of miners who sought better opportunities in southern Ontario, 11 resigned and there remained 26 members, that is, 22 men and 4 women. A primary concern was the religious life of the Ukrainian community.[253] Ukrainian Catholic and Orthodox clergy visited Val-d'Or only three or four times a year. In the years up to 1950, this arrangement worked well according to the local community that was composed largely of Ukrainian Catholics but with a significant minority of Ukrainian Orthodox. The new DP immigrants were almost all Ukrainian Catholics.

The SUM branch organized the petition to Bishop Isidore Borecky of the Ukrainian Catholic Church in Toronto for a parish priest for Val-d'Or, Malartic and Rouyn-Noranda. There was a fear that the new immigrants would become targets for missionary efforts by various other Protestant churches as happened among the first wave of Ukrainian pioneers in western Canada. A significant number of the DP families made the decision to live and work in Val-d'Or after their contracts expired and felt that a church was a vital part of their community life. In October, 1952, Father Lev Chayka was appointed as the Ukrainian Catholic parish priest residing in Val-d'Or. He was born in Ukraine in 1923 and came to Canada in 1948. He completed his theological studies in Montreal and was ordained on 4 May, 1952.[254] He spoke French and was to serve also in Rouyn, Noranda, Malartic, Lac Castagnier, Perron, Amos and Duparquet. Father Chayka arrived on 28 November, 1952 and began to organize the parish.[255] Fr. Chayka later claimed that there were 375 families in Val-d'Or and 50 families in Malartic. He called a general meeting soon after his arrival and began plans to build a Ukrainian Catholic church.[256]

In 1954, the SUM branch lost more members. At least 11 members left Val-d'Or, 8 left for Toronto and 4 for Windsor, Ontario. A survey was conducted among the youth and 39 children and youth were identified, that is, those born between 1935 and 1948. A Ridna Shkola (Ukrainian language school) was organized with the SUM branch but with the departure of the teachers for southern Ontario in 1954, the school ceased. The branch organized a drama group and a choir. Special interest groups were also organized - sewing, book club, sport, library. Plays were performed that attracted the entire Ukrainian community. The plays were rehearsed in private homes and performed in rented facilities. In 1952, the first Ukrainian language radio program was broadcast on the local radio station CKVD. The program that cost over $800.00 every

**Youth Members of the Ukrainian Youth Organization (CYM) with Michael Muzychka**, circa 1956. Some members were also students at the CYM Ukrainian School. *Photo credit:* Myron Momryk

year continued for a half-hour every Sunday morning for over ten years. The program broadcast local news, music and also anti-communist political editorials from the Ukrainian nationalist newspaper, *Homin Ukrainy*. However, the lack of a hall or a regular meeting place seriously limited SUM branch activities.

Relations with the larger French Canadian and English Canadian communities were amicable although there were isolated incidences of misunderstanding. One major complaint among the Ukrainians was the unfortunate habit among some French Canadians to categorize all recent immigrants as 'Poloks' or 'Polonais' obliging the Ukrainians to

**Stefan Momryk, announcing Ukrainian Radio Program**, CKVD, circa 1960.
*Photo credit:* Myron Momryk

explain their separate identity and history when anyone cared to listen. The English Canadians tended to consider the Ukrainians as 'Russians' and again, it was constantly required to explain their Ukrainian identity. The Ukrainian nationalism of the new arrivals and the continuing Cold War obliged the Ukrainian DPs to emphasize their national identity as different from the Russian and Polish identity and especially different and in opposition to Soviet Communism.

The early 1950s were the most active years in the history of the community. The arrival of the new immigrants with their hopes and dreams brought a new sense of activity and dynamism to the community.

By this time, the main factions in the community were well defined. Most members from each community knew who belonged to the 'other side' and in some cases, parents pointed out to their children who were the 'communists' when they encountered them on the streets. The nationalist community included members of the Ukrainian Catholic parish, SUM and UNF. The pro-communist community continued their activities but limited their public events to a minimum due to the Cold War environment and the open hostility of Premier Maurice Duplessis and his provincial government. There was also a small but unorganized group of Canadian-born families of Ukrainian origin who did not participate in any of the organized events in the community. Their attitudes and experiences were based on their Canadian background and tended to view the political rivalries and disputes among the older and more recent immigrants with some amusement and general incomprehension.

**Ukrainian Drama Group**, 1955. Plays were performed at the UNF Hall during the 1950s. In December of some years, a short play was performed as part of the annual St. Nicholas concert.
Standing, from left to right: Ivan Taniuk, Mrs. Worona, Stephan Tkachyshyn (?), Mrs. Katharina Puszczynski, Michael Muzychka, Mrs. Mackiw, Paul Zbihlyj, Mrs. Tkachyshyn, Steve Momryk; sitting, Natalie Andrusyshyn, Peter Sarachman. All of these individuals later moved from Val-d'Or to southern Ontario, New York City and Saskatoon, Saskatchewan. *Photo credit:* E. Ostapchuk fonds, LAC, C010767571.

## THE SCHOOL QUESTION

### 1948-1956

In the early 1950s, the first 'baby boomers' began to enter the local school system. This particular experience reflected the general relationship with the local Anglophone and Francophone communities. In general, the Francophone community was concerned with preserving their own language and culture. Their local community and religious organizations were structured to maintain maximum local autonomy and independence. They concentrated their social, cultural and religious efforts almost entirely within their own community. Although there were initial efforts made by the local Roman Catholic Church to welcome other Roman Catholics from the immigrant communities, there were no French Canadian community organizations whose efforts were specifically directed at welcoming and integrating the new immigrants into their community.

The Anglophone community was very small in numbers but sought to develop and maintain a range of local community organizations including youth associations. To supplement their numbers, they actively recruited members from among English-speaking Francophones and especially from among the European immigrant groups.[257] The local Baptist Church under the leadership of Rev. Lorne Heron made special efforts to attract youth to various church-sponsored social and religious events. The English-speaking Boy Scout organization welcomed members from all ethnocultural groups. For most of this period, the local French Canadian community had no organizations that welcomed the new immigrants other than the Roman Catholic Church. From the local Ukrainian community perspective, the fundamental difference was the defensive and isolationist attitude of the majority Québécois organized community and the generally open and welcoming attitude of the smaller Anglophone community.[258]

In regards to the choice of school systems, the older Ukrainian immigrants advised the recent immigrants to send their children to the local English Protestant elementary school since the level of teaching was supposedly higher than in the French Catholic system. A member of the Ukrainian community had already served on the Protestant School Board.[259] The new immigrants were informed by the older generation of immigrants that career opportunities for their children were much better if they graduated from the English-language school system. Graduates from English-language schools could apply to universities across Canada and even in the United States whereas graduates from the local French-language schools were limited to the classical colleges and universities in Quebec only. Some Ukrainian families, who could afford the expense, sent their children to schools in Toronto to ensure that they obtained the best available education.[260]

There were already examples of individual success stories among the immigrants that encouraged the Ukrainian parents. Frank Belle, the son of an Italian immigrant and mining camp cook, completed a graduate degree at McGill despite having lost the use of his sight at an early age as a result of a kitchen accident.[261] John Petrushka, the son of Slovak immigrants, received scholarships and awards at Bishops University and continued his studies at the graduate level in the United States.[262] These and other success stories were regularly reported in the local English-language newspaper, *The Star* that encouraged and motivated the more ambitious immigrant families in the community.

Also, the French Catholic school system had difficulty in coping with the increase in their own 'baby boom' enrolments and were not particularly interested in receiving children from immigrant families. The question of religion played a dominant role in the selection of schools. The French Catholic administrators, who were mostly members of Roman Catholic religious orders, insisted that all new students must be Roman Catholic.[263] Recent Ukrainian immigrants who were Ukrainian (Greek) Orthodox or Ukrainian (Greek) Catholic were discouraged from attending. This informal policy was a continuation of the long tradition of avoiding close contacts with non-French Canadians and other 'foreigners' that may undermine the ages-long struggle to preserve their language and traditions. Eventually a compromise was reached and the Ukrainian Catholic students were enrolled in the English-language

Roman Catholic school. Others chose to send their children to Queen Elizabeth, the English-language Protestant school. This decision directed the children of immigrants into the Anglophone educational system, a primary institution of cultural integration and established a tradition that permanently shaped the local Ukrainian community. These children in both English-language school systems were educated in the Anglophone tradition however many became tri-lingual having a working knowledge of English, Ukrainian and French.[264]

# BUILDING THE UKRAINIAN CATHOLIC CHURCH

## 1953-1954

In early 1953, Father Leo Chayka began to lay the foundations for a parish organization.[265] At first, Church services were held in St. Sauveur, the Roman Catholic parish church in the afternoons after the Roman Catholic masses were celebrated. The parish included 95 families although not all were active in the parish.[266] Father Chayka had as his role models the early pioneer missionaries who built Ukrainian Catholic churches across western Canada. A parish meeting was held and a decision made to build a church.

A Church Building Committee was formed and the building of the new church began on 1 May, 1954. It was estimated that the building of the Church would cost $25,000-$30,000.[267] Since the parish did not have among its members the required specialists and professionals such as accountants and engineers to assist in the building and administering of the church, the parish priest had to assume by choice and by circumstance total responsibility for the project. Fundraising was the most important aspect of the project. In a community of new immigrants who were attempting to establish themselves, constant fund raising during the next years created stress and friction that in some cases, permanently alienated a few individuals and their families from the parish.

The community especially the younger members from the SUM branch gave generously of their time, energy and funds. After working an eight-hour day in the local mines, some miners would come and work on the building of the church.[268] The municipal administration donated the land for the church. A local mining company donated the electrical wiring and the services of their electricians to wire the building. Other local individuals and companies made donations of goods and services. The church, Protection of the Blessed Virgin Mary, was finally completed and officially dedicated by Bishop Isidore Borecky on 4 September, 1955. The first Divine Liturgy was held on Ukrainian Christmas,

6-7 January, 1955. The building of the Church had cost $55,000.[269] To finance the building of the Church, various fund-raising activities were organized. Lotteries for automobiles, dances and Christmas caroling became part of the annual cycle of events dedicated to fund-raising for the Church. Fr. Chayka's career was distinguished by his constant fund-raising campaigns that continued for many more years. He would solicit donations from all sectors of the Ukrainian community including individuals that attended the Russian Orthodox Church and other individuals who were known to be members of the left-wing organizations. He also extended his fund-raising activities to the Anglophone and French Canadian population.

One of the goals in building the Church was to unite all anti-communist Ukrainians both Catholic and Orthodox. This plan however partly failed when the local Russian community announced in May, 1954, their goal to build a Russian Orthodox Church.[270] The St. Nicholas Church

**Construction of the Ukrainian Catholic Church**, July, 1954.
Katherine Slobodian, Marie Kluczkowsky, John Kluczkowsky, Steve Momryk, Nicholas Lytwyn, Stephan Tkachyshyn, Rev. Leo Chayka, Hryhorij Diachyk, John Nastasiak, Paul Koshilka, Mike Mackiw, Dmytro Romanyshyn, Harry Zahoruk, Theodore Worona, John Ferdorynec, John Kuzma, Peter Kordan, John Smoly, Mike Andrusyshyn, Paul Zbihly, Walter Lemyk, John Chmelowsky, Joseph Kluchkowsky, Nicholas Kruk, Philippe Andrusyshyn, John Mynych, Peter Sarachman, Mike Muzychka.
Photo credit: La Société d'histoire et de généalogie de Val-d'Or

was built and consecrated on 19 December, 1954.[271] The church was built in front of the home of Theodore Koulomozine, the Russian community leader. This small Russian Orthodox Church attracted a small number of Ukrainian families that originated from Volyn, Bukovyna and central Ukraine. This parish also included members from various other ethno-cultural groups.

The large majority of the Ukrainian Orthodox families did attend the new Ukrainian Catholic Church and were regular members of the parish. However, there were occasions when parish disagreements and disputes quickly became identified as issues between the Catholics and the Orthodox with the Orthodox supporting the more traditional customs and practices. In the Orthodox tradition, it was the parish that 'owned' the church and decided all matters relating to the building and property. In the Ukrainian Catholic tradition in Canada, it was the Ukrainian Catholic Bishop in Toronto that 'owned' the property and church building and important decisions had to be referred to Toronto. At the other end of the religious spectrum, there were also individual Canadian-born members of the parish who raised questions about the observance of traditional religious holidays in particular Christmas, that they preferred to celebrate on December 25 with the other Catholic and Protestant churches rather than on the traditional January 7. This variety in membership did not ease the new parish priest's role and responsibilities.

**Divine Liturgy at the Ukrainian Catholic Church**, circa 1960
*Photo credit:* Myron Momryk

## CONTINUITY AND CHANGE

### 1954-1967

Many of the Ukrainian Displaced Persons who arrived as miners after the Second World War, completed their one-year contract and left for southern Ontario. This was especially true of the single men in the community who had greater freedom of mobility. Others stayed for two, three or more years but also left when they received news of warmer climates and better paying jobs in the Toronto area.[272] The Duparquet mine closed in April, 1955 and some of the Ukrainians left for the Toronto area while a few families settled in Rouyn-Noranda and Val-d'Or. Some individuals continued to live at the former mine site.[273]

The Ukrainian left-wing community continued to hold various fund-raising events at their hall on 11th street but without any public political speeches. Some of these events were reported in the Ukrainian left-wing press along with the names of donors that averaged about 20 donors. Funds were raised to support the newspapers, *The Canadian Tribune, Novo Vremia, Vestnik, and Ukrainske Zhyttia (Ukrainian Life)*. The number of events declined and only a few were held during the summer months.[274] Some fund-raising took place at family events that were reported to the RCMP through anonymous letters.[275] Surveillance by the RCMP continued and lists of local subscribers to the Ukrainian left-wing press were compiled.[276]

There were also other events during these years that were not reported in the press but were generally known among the community. There were mine and traffic accidents, a few suicides, some in dramatic circumstances in public places. Also, when a few Ukrainian 'old timers' passed away destitute, the cost of their funerals was paid through 'public assistance'. Funerals were held in local Protestant churches, Roman Catholic, Ukrainian Catholic and Russian Orthodox Churches. Funerals of members of the Ukrainian left-wing organizations were usually held at the Russian Orthodox Church.

In 1956 and 1957, the Displaced Persons who arrived in the years 1948-52, applied and received their Canadian Citizenship papers.[277]

With the Canadian citizenship, the new citizens felt that they now had a greater freedom of movement. Also, mine accidents among the newly arrived immigrants encouraged some to seek safer occupations.[278] However, positive descriptions of the life of miners in Abitibi appeared from time to time and one such report was broadcast by Radio Canada International to Soviet Ukraine.[279]

In 1952, there were 37 members in the SUM branch, but in 1955, only 20 members remained. Also, some of the older pre-war immigrants left for other parts of Canada. After 1953, the UNF branch had only 15 members. The limited number of members resulted in the election of the same individuals to the executive for many years. For example, Wasyl Poremskyj was the president of the UNF branch for many decades until the late 1960s.[280] Because of the reduced numbers in the community and the relatively older average age, the annual cycle of activities were reduced to St. Nicholas Day, Taras Shevchenko Day and National Heroes Day. In 1954, the UNF branch agreed to hold joint events with the newer SUM branch in the UNF hall.

In 1954, a youth section of the SUM Branch was formed with 23 children. These children were born as part of the post-war 'baby boom' during the years 1946-50. Mychailo (Michael) Muzychka, a miner, volunteered his services as a teacher and a Ukrainian School was established with these children as pupils. Mr. Muzychka was an active member of the Organization of Ukrainian Nationalists, Bandera faction. The SUM branch made an informal arrangement to use the newly built Ukrainian Catholic Church hall for their activities including the Ukrainian School.

However, as families moved to southern Ontario, the number of children declined and the youth section of the SUM Branch had only 12 members in 1956. The Ukrainian School taught the Ukrainian language, history and geography. Classes were held for three hours on Saturdays. The teacher, Mykhailo Muzychka, would often arrive to teach after completing an eight-hour shift at the mine.[281]

Most SUM Branch meetings were held to commemorate Ukrainian political events and discuss school matters. Because of the declining membership, the SUM Branch concentrated its activities on supporting the Ukrainian School and the Ukrainian radio program on the local radio station, CKVD.[282]

By 1955-56, Father Chayka began to build a Ukrainian Catholic Church in Rouyn-Noranda. In 1957, he acquired a campsite on Lac Simard near Val-d'Or as a recreational area for his parish. A parish residence was built in Val-d'Or in 1962.[283] Although he initiated a few parish organizations in Val-d'Or such as Boy Scouts, Ukrainian Catholic Women's League, Ukrainian Catholic Brotherhood, Ukrainian Catholic Youth, his activities often took him to other local towns. From 1958, he undertook part-time graduate studies at the University of Ottawa and commuted regularly between Ottawa and Val-d'Or.[284] Without a permanent and stable leadership, these organizations remained essentially as dormant organizations revived by the parish priest for special church functions. To reach his dispersed parishioners scattered across northwestern Quebec, Father

**Ukrainian community tribute to Reverend Leo Chayka at the UNF Hall**, November 22, 1956.
Reverend Chayka (3rd row in the middle) was the founding priest of the Ukrainian Catholic Church in Val-d'Or.
*Photo credit:* La Société d'histoire et de généalogie de Val-d'Or

Chayka began his own radio program on the local CKVD radio station broadcasting on Sunday mornings.[285]

The Val-d'Or municipal authorities evaluated the UNF hall valued at $5,600 for property tax purposes and began to submit tax invoices of $42.00 that, for the small membership, was an inconvenient burden. The UNF branch succeeded in arguing their case that the UNF hall was also used as a Ukrainian Orthodox Church when missionary priests travelled through the region. The UNF hall was exempted from property tax as a Church.[286]

The issue of religion emerged again when the school tax had to be paid. Seven Ukrainian families sent their children to the Protestant school system but as Ukrainian (Greek) Catholics were also required to pay the Catholic school tax. The issue dragged on for several months in 1958 until they officially registered their religion as Ukrainian (Greek) Orthodox.[287]

**UNF members**, Val-d'Or Branch, 1957.
Wasyl Poremski (center, middle row) was President of this Branch for many years.
*Photo credit:* Stephanie Borsuk MacArthur

The Russian Orthodox priest, Rev. Fedor Ustutschenkov died in 1957 at the age of 67 years and he was buried in the Protestant Cemetery in Val-d'Or. He was the first parish priest of the Russian Orthodox Church.[288] He was replaced in 1958 by Rev. David Shevchenko, who also served the Russian Orthodox parish in Rouyn-Noranda and other missions.[289] Rev. Shevchenko usually travelled to various centers across Abitibi by bus to perform religious services and stayed overnight with his parishioners.

The years 1953 until 1957 were a period of out-migration for many families from the Ukrainian community.[290] Among those who departed on October 2, 1956 was a miner, Ludwik Mackow (Matskiw), who was returning to his wife and daughter in Soviet Ukraine after 29 years in Canada. A farewell party was organized by the left-wing community and 14 individuals made a donation to the press fund.[291]

After William Warwaruk passed away in 1954, his widow reportedly married Joe Lisow (Lisovsky) who was a long-time boarder in their house. Warwaruk's daughter, Virginia (Vera), born in Val-d'Or on 3 January, 1939, attended McGill University in Montreal at the same time as Jennie Smoly, also from Val-d'Or. However, during the summer of 1956, friends were invited to attend a farewell dinner at their home in Val-d'Or because the family including Virginia and her brother, Richard, was moving to Montreal. But within a short time, Jennie Smoly received a postcard from Virginia in July, 1956 that she was on a ship and heading for Soviet Ukraine. In Soviet Ukraine, Vera Lisovskaya continued her university studies and received a PhD in Marine Biology. She married, had a family and lived and worked in Odessa. Some contacts were maintained between Virginia and her friends in Canada.[292] Her brother, Richard Lisovsky, also born in Val-d'Or, completed his education in Odessa. He began his work as a scientist in 1969 and, for 30 years, he worked with the Ukrainian Scientific Centre of Ecology of the Sea in Odessa.[293]

Almost all Ukrainian families in Val-d'Or maintained contacts with relatives in Ukraine through correspondence and the sending of parcels. These contacts began for many recent immigrants only after the death of the Soviet leader, Joseph Stalin on 5 March, 1953. There were jokes that the local Kresge department store dressed half of Poland and western

25th **Wedding Anniversary of Mr. and Mrs. Michael Borsuk**. UNF Hall, September 1958.
*Photo credit:* Stephanie Borsuk MacArthur

Ukraine. The return letters from Soviet Ukraine included only basic information, no political comments and always requests for more parcels. Some individuals from the second wave of Ukrainian immigration that arrived in Canada prior to the Second World War, considered returning to Soviet Ukraine but the various restrictions on the transportation of personal property, the place of settlement in Soviet Ukraine and other Soviet governmental requirements discouraged them from leaving.

In June, 1955, an effort was made to renovate the Labour Hall on 11th Street. A carpenter was hired to repair and repaint the building. Much of the work was done by volunteers from the WBA, AUUC and the FRC in the evenings.[294]

Events in the Soviet Union had an impact in the local left-wing community in Val-d'Or. When the Soviet Premier, Nikita Khrushchev denounced Joseph Stalin in his famous speech at the CPSU Congress in Moscow in 1956, questions were raised in Val-d'Or. Oscar Roy, member of the Communist Party of Canada and frequent candidate in provincial and federal elections, spoke on this topic at a banquet at the Labour Hall on 13 May, 1956. He claimed that Joseph Stalin had too much power in his hands and this resulted in his making serious political and economic mistakes.[295] This controversial news about Stalin spread some confusion among the pro-communist members of the local community but a core group remained and continued their activities mostly fund-raising for their newspapers and various political causes in Winnipeg and Toronto.

According to the RCMP reports, the local branch of the AUUC organized only a few activities. In February, 1958, the AUUC branch had only six members.[296] In September, 1958, the AUUC-FRC Hall was sold to the Royal Canadian Legion Branch.[297] This hall was used by all the left-wing ethnocultural groups in Val-d'Or but in previous years the hall was seldom used. Reminders of the Cold War continued to be evident in Val-d'Or with the arrival in January, 1957, of twenty-one Hungarian refugees who escaped after the Hungarian Uprising of 1956.[298] The Soviet suppression of the Hungarian Uprising and the failure of the United States and other western democratic nations to support this uprising, obliged many in the local Ukrainian nationalist community to re-evaluate their attitude towards Canada and Ukraine. From this experience, many Ukrainian Displaced Persons who arrived after the Second World War realized that they could not return to Ukraine and now had to dedicate their lives to living and working in Canada. This attitude became more pronounced after the assassination of Stepan Bandera in Munich, Germany on 15 October, 1959 by a Soviet agent who later confessed to his crime. Stepan Bandera was a leader of the Ukrainian nationalist movement since the pre-Second World War years and the SUM Branch in Val-d'Or was part of this movement.

By 1956, the Ukrainian nationalist community and especially the Canadian-born children began to feel that their future was definitely in Canada and thoughts of returning to Ukraine began to fade. This attitude was emphasized in a statement made by Rev. Chayka in May, 1956 that the Ukrainians were Canadians now and not political exiles.[299] At various formal events, local French Canadian politicians encouraged the Ukrainian community to follow in the tradition of political involvement established by the pioneer Ukrainians in western Canada.[300] There were attempts by various government-sponsored organizations to establish English-language schools for the new immigrants. These efforts were met by initial enthusiasm but faded after a few sessions due to shift-work, large classes and inadequate teaching methods. From their first years in Canada, some individuals made attempts to learn the English-language on their own especially when it became necessary to pass the various tests to obtain their driving permits.

The sense of Canadianism was enhanced among the Ukrainian community with the news that the Hon. Michael Starr, a Canadian of Ukrainian origin was appointed to the John Diefenbaker Cabinet as Minister of Labour in June, 1957. This news made a profound impression on the local community and stimulated their interest in Canadian politics.[301] At the local and provincial levels, some members of the Ukrainian community voted for the Union Nationale Party because of the strong anti-communist stand of Premier Maurice Duplessis. Some voted for the Liberal Party at the national level because it was under this government that they were allowed to immigrate to Canada after the Second World War. After the election of John Diefenbaker and the Progressive Conservative government, many of the Ukrainian nationalists voted for this political party because of the anti-communist speeches of Mike Starr and John Diefenbaker. The pro-communist section was encouraged to vote by their press for candidates from the Labour-Progressive Party.

After several years of struggle to establish themselves, the Ukrainian immigrants began to feel more comfortable in Val-d'Or. The town had acquired many of the municipal services that made life more agreeable. Most of the main roads were paved with sidewalks and new subdivisions were built at the edges of the town. From their first years, some Ukrainians bought automobiles which gave them more mobility in Val-d'Or and enabled them to travel to the larger centers in Quebec and Ontario. Many now owned or built their own homes. In several cases, they built small apartment buildings for additional income. These buildings were the result of group efforts where the miners assisted each other with pouring cement for basements and with carpentry, working in evenings and on weekends.

In some cases, the selection of new homes was determined by their proximity to the bus routes that took the miners to and from work. Others walked from their homes to work at the Sigma and Lamaque Mines. In general, most Ukrainians lived in the central and eastern part of the town. The 'Ukrainian' geography of Val-d'Or was determined by the usual landmarks of main buildings and streets but more importantly, by the residences, stores and buildings of their Ukrainian and East European inhabitants. From the Ukrainian perspective, Val-d'Or was very similar to a large Ukrainian village overlaid on the geography of the town. In February, 1960, a request was submitted to municipal authorities to have a street name changed to Bishop Isidore Borecky Street.[302] The Québécois and other inhabitants formed an important and very obvious part of this human geography but more in a peripheral and secondary role in their daily activities.

Ukrainian community life was centered around the Ukrainian Catholic Church and its hall and the UNF hall. The two grocery stores operated by members of the community also became 'drop-in' centers where local news and events could be discussed.[303] During the 1950s, the annual cycle of events continued with various social and political events added or postponed depending on the enthusiasm and dedication of individual community members. For the younger generation of males, the poolrooms and bowling alleys operated by a few Ukrainian businessmen became social centers especially in winter.

St. Nicholas Day was celebrated in the Ukrainian tradition in early December as separate from Christmas that was celebrated as a religious holiday on 6 January every year. This celebration distinguished the Ukrainian community from the other Catholic East European groups and from the larger English and French communities. The New Years Eve celebrations known as 'Malanka' were also community events in which the entire non-communist community participated. On these occasions, various French Canadian politicians from the municipal or provincial levels were invited to participate as honoured guests in the banquets and dinners. These events were usually concluded with a dance.

In the summer, the Ukrainian community participated in parade in honour of the St. Jean Baptiste Day celebrated on 24 June every year. Some of the other ethnocultural groups especially the Polish community also participated in this parade. A truck would be decorated and participants dressed in Ukrainian embroidered shirts. Ukrainian 'princesses' were chosen to ride in convertible cars waving to the crowds. During one celebration in the late 1950s, Rev. Chayka was able to obtain horses and a few men dressed as Cossacks rode them in the parade to the delight of the local population.

Individual members of the community gained some prominence in the local press. For example, Miss Olga Borsuk was a candidate in 1956 in the annual Miss Val d'Or contest organized by the Fire Department.[304] In May, 1956, Jenny Smoly was one of two students who won a trip to visit Ottawa through the local Rotary Club.[305] At the UNF hall, a small dance group was formed in May, 1957 to perform Ukrainian dances.[306] A few individuals were members of the local Val d'Or-Bourlamaque Chess Club and in 1959, Mike Muzychka won the chess trophy.[307]

In October, 1957, ads for television sets began to appear in the local newspapers and CKRN began to broadcast from Rouyn-Noranda on 25 December, 1957.[308] There were only two television channels, with French-language broadcasts from Rouyn and English-language broadcasts from Timmins. Many Ukrainian families purchased the sets and interest in television programs kept many families at home especially in winter and with time, influenced the decline in attendance at events in the UNF hall. Also, the television programs introduced the Ukrainian community to the local Québécois culture with sports especially hockey and political programs.

Some social and recreational activities were shared with the larger East European community. Although the Ukrainian community declined in numbers, the larger number of Poles, Byelorussians, Russians, Slovaks and other Slavic groups formed a more numerous and broader community that acted as a supportive environment for each other. This was especially true when anyone from the East European groups suffered an accident or fatal mining accident. The loss was felt by everyone since most miners from the East European groups knew each other and their families.

Almost every Ukrainian family grew flowers and kept a vegetable garden. Individual Ukrainians were noted in the local press as excellent gardeners.[309] The produce from the gardens was preserved in jars for the winter. Some families made their own preserved cabbage (sauerkraut) and pickled herring. In August, whole families would travel to the local woods to pick blueberries that were made into pies or stored for the winter. In September, it was the mushroom season and they were also preserved either by drying or in jars. Some Ukrainians became avid fishermen and a few took advantage of the hunting season in the fall.

The miners developed their own work culture that also had an influence on the customs and habits of the larger community. The miners who spoke French, English and a variety of East European languages evolved their own 'miner's language' based on the names of mining equipment

**Ukrainian Princesses**, St Jean Baptiste Parade, circa June, 1958.
Stephanie Borsuk, Judy Kruk, Diane Koshilka. *Photo credit:* Stephanie Borsuk MacArthur

and their use. The Ukrainian miners quickly learned a basic vocabulary of French and English words that was adequate for their work. Among themselves, the Ukrainian miners spoke their own language and generally understood miners who spoke the other East European languages. Because underground work at the mines was dangerous, the miners developed a form a loyalty to the mine not unlike sailors to their ships. When the miners went on strikes called by their union, they went but only reluctantly. But they all took their turns on the picket lines and the hourly pay increases were relatively small. There were cases where individual Ukrainian miners refused to participate in the strike and had to be physically restrained by other striking miners on the picket lines from entering the mine property to go to work. Involvement in union activities by the Ukrainian DP miners was minimal due to the union reputation for pro-socialist activities and the general ineffectiveness of the unions.

Throughout the history of the community, there were always a small number of single men who developed their own lifestyle familiar to most frontier mining towns. Many lived in boarding and rooming houses while others lived as boarders in the homes of Ukrainian and other East European families. Some fell prey to hard-drinking habits that they were never able to overcome and they were perceived as a negative influence on the reputation of the community. Practical jokes and horseplay at the mine resulted in a few cases in accidents and court cases. Sometimes jokes were played on individuals at community events that were remembered for many years. In the late 1950s, individual families purchased or built cottages (known as camps) on the local lakes.

A few individuals travelled to southern Ontario during their holidays to visit their friends who had left Val-d'Or in previous years and also to investigate employment prospects. The economic recession that began in 1956 and continued until 1963 raised the level of unemployment and discouraged the miners from moving at that time. In Val-d'Or, 20% of the labour force was unemployed in January, 1958.[310] Some postponed their decision to move to the Toronto area and never left Val-d'Or. When the mines in Chibougamau opened in the mid-1950s, a few individuals and their families left to take advantage of the new opportunities. In individual cases, a few miners worked in Chibougamau but left their families in Val-d'Or. Other individuals and families left for new mine jobs in Elliot Lake and the Northwest Territories.

In Val-d'Or, job opportunities for the younger members of the community were few unless they were related to the mining industry. There were individual students who attempted to follow a career in mining by enrolling in the provincial school of mining in Haileybury, Ontario. Throughout the 1950s and into the 1960s, several younger members of the community joined the Canadian armed forces. Steve Bizyk, 19 years old, joined the RCAF as a pilot in July, 1959.[311] The Val-d'Or region was a fertile ground for recruitment and there were 300 enlistments from the general population from 1954 until 1957.[312] The Royal Canadian Army Cadet Corps at the local schools provided a pool of potential recruits. The Cadet Corps also gave an opportunity for some individuals to develop leadership skills.[313]

In the years 1957-62, four Ukrainian families including Father Chayka's parents arrived from Poland and were fully integrated into the community.[314] Michael Steranka was sponsored by his brother, Wasyl Steranka, who arrived as a Displaced Person in the late 1940s. Joseph Kliuchkowsky, a Ukrainian miner, sponsored the arrival of his wife and son, John Kluczkowski, from Poland that he had not seen since the late 1920s. Both Michael Steranka and John Kluczkowski were veterans of the Ukrainian Insurgent Army and Michael Steranka was sentenced to ten years in prison in Poland for his membership in the Ukrainian Insurgent Army.[315] However, following the trend already established, John Kluczkowski and his family, soon moved to Oshawa.

Another person that left Val-d'Or in June, 1960 was Molly Hawryluk, a teacher at the Queen Elizabeth School. A farewell dinner was organized for her and other teachers leaving Val-d'Or.[316]

In the 1961 census, there were 216 Ukrainians in a total population of 15,541 in Val-d'Or. Of this total number, 12,813 were of French Canadian origin, 940 were of British origin and 1,756 were of European origin. In Abitibi County, there were 329 Ukrainians.[317] The 'baby boom' generation was now completing the local high schools and planning to enter post-secondary institutions. Inevitably this meant that the students would have to leave Val-d'Or for the larger urban centers.

Students who were born in the early 1940s were already attending post-secondary institutions. In 1959, Irene Kruk graduated in nursing in St. Catharines, Ontario.[318] In 1961, Diane Koshilka won a scholarship to attend teachers college.[319] Marcel (Wasyl) Lesyk, from Amos, completed classical studies in Trois Rivieres and was working for the rehabilitation of juvenile delinquents. He was the only Ukrainian student from the Abitibi region who graduated from the French Canadian post-secondary school system.[320] Nick Andrusyshyn won a scholarship in 1962 to attend the University of Waterloo.[321] In 1963, Steve Bizyk enrolled at the Michigan Institute of Technology after one year at the Provincial Institute of Mining in Haileybury.[322]

In a few cases, plans to enroll the children in a university persuaded the entire family to migrate to southern Ontario. Also, a few miners were now in their late thirties or early forties and began to experience health problems related to their years of heavy physical work in the mines. They saw this move as their last opportunity to obtain better employment in the larger manufacturing centers following other families who had left in previous years.

The SUM Branch continued their activities mostly administering the Ukrainian School. Following other Ukrainian families, Mychailo Muzychka, a community leader, moved with his family to Toronto[323] and, as a result, there was a significant decline in activities. Attempts were made to continue the Ukrainian school in private homes and at the Queen Elizabeth School.[324]

The rising Québécois nationalism at the local level also had an indirect effect on the decision to move to southern Ontario. The local anglophone community was relatively small compared to the steadily increasing Québécois population. Some of the East European immigrants knew that they were too old or simply unable to successfully integrate into the Québécois community. Among the younger generation, there was a more optimistic attitude. For example, Diane Koshilka, attending the University of Western Ontario in London, Ontario, appeared before the Royal Commission on Bilingualism and Biculturalism in April, 1964 and spoke on the benefits of learning French.[325]

On 8 October, 1961, the UNF branch celebrated its 25th Anniversary. Representatives of the UNF National Executive visited Val-d'Or and took part in the celebrations. The day began with a Divine Liturgy at the Ukrainian Catholic Church, a concert in the afternoon and a banquet in the evening.[326] At the concert held at the Capital Theatre in Bourlamaque, a 50-voice mixed choir from Sudbury UNF Branch performed.[327] In following years, this choir returned frequently to perform before audiences in Val-d'Or. The UNF Women's League branch celebrated its 25th anniversary in 1963 with twenty two members.[328]

The Val-d'Or Branch of the Ukrainian Catholic Women's League participated in a regional conference in Rouyn-Noranda in 1962 and the participants were: M. Kruk, A. Lytvyn, O. Chayka (mother of Fr. Chayka), N. Andrusyshyn, M. Zbihly, E. Borsuk, P. Sikorsky.[329]

RCMP surveillance of the Ukrainian left-wing community continued but it was reported that local activities were limited to fund-raising for the press. In one report in June, 1962, the RCMP noted that no new annual elections were held because there were very few members.[330] The local branch of the Federation of Russian Canadians ceased its activities in 1961.

The Cuban Missile Crisis of October, 1962 was a reminder of the continuing Cold War. The local Royal Canadian Air Force base was used as an advance base by jet fighters from Uplands and North Bay. In 1956 and 1961, the runway was extended and in November, 1962, the first CF-101 jet fighters were stationed in Val-d'Or. During October, large United States Air Force planes arrived at the military airport in Val-d'Or. In 1964, the local RCAF base received nuclear weapons from the United States that were stored on the base and guarded by members of the United States Air Force.[331] For several years, American military families lived in the area and their children attended the local Protestant schools. The air base became an advance air post and the control tower was operated by the RCAF.[332]

From an examination of the names of the SUM executive elected each year during 1959-62, the same names kept reappearing. Because of misunderstandings with the parish priest, the SUM branch no longer had access to the Church parish hall for their activities that were now held in private homes. For example, the Ukrainian School was conducted for a short time at the Queen Elizabeth Elementary School and in a private home of one of the SUM members. On 21 October, 1963, the SUM branch was formally dissolved and closed on 27 December, 1963. The archives were sent to Toronto and eventually preserved at the Archives of Ontario. In the last year of its activities, the SUM branch had five adult members and four youth members.[333] In the next few years, the last former members moved to southern Ontario. At this time, a number of Ukrainian families including Mike Muzychka and his family, moved to the Toronto area as the national economy began to recover from the recession. Mike Muzyczka worked at the headquarters of the SUM organization in Toronto and then worked in a factory. He passed away in Toronto on 13 March, 2005 and was buried in St. Volodymyr Cemetery in Oakville.[334]

The miners were again reminded of the dangerous work in the mines when news was received in August, 1964 that Bill Fedorko was killed in a mining accident near Rouyn. He was 24 years old and from Perron. The funeral service was held in St. Sauveur Roman Catholic Church.[335]

The achievements of the Ukrainian community were also noted in the local English-language press. The John Smoly and John Kluczkowski families celebrated a double 25th Wedding Anniversary in March, 1965 confirming their status as being among the first Ukrainian pioneers in the area. Also Jennie Mary Smoly received her Doctorate in biochemistry from McGill University in June, 1965 which was also a noted achievement.[336] Jennie Smoly continued her distinguished scientific career in the United States.[337]

The numerical decline of the Anglophone and European communities was brought to everyone's attention when the local radio station CKVD decided in July, 1965 to end English-language broadcasting.[338] The local residents now had to listen to the province-wide CBC English network originating from Montreal. Among the ethnocultural groups, Branch 12 of the Canadian Slovak League, established in 1936, was dissolved in 1969. By 1974, there were very few English-language movies shown in the Capital Theatre because of the low ticket sales and there was a danger that they would cease entirely.[339] In 1980, the St. Andrew's Anglican Church joined with the Val d'Or United Church to form the Golden Valley Church, a shared United Church/Anglican ministry. The Golden Valley Church remained the only English-speaking church in Val-d'Or. With the Quiet Revolution in Quebec, the rise of Québécois nationalism and a general secular life-style among the population, attendance at the Roman Catholic Churches in the Val-d'Or area declined to the point that by 2000 only the St. Sauveur Church was holding regular Church services. The other Roman Catholic churches including the Church in Jacola were closed and sold.

The decline in the number of parishioners in the Ukrainian Catholic Church placed an added financial burden on the remaining members. Already by 1965, the parish had difficulty in maintaining its

**The last mortgage payment for the building of the Ukrainian Catholic Church with Reverend Leo Chayka,** 1967. *From left to right:* Nicolas Lytwyn, Reverend Leo Chayka, Gregory Chayka and a representative of a local bank. *Photo credit:* La Société d'histoire et de généalogie de Val-d'Or

self-sustaining financial position. The need to meet financial payments on the Church mortgage perpetuated stress and conflict in the parish. As a result of one of these confrontations, Rev. Chayka was transferred to Montreal and he was replaced by Rev. Yaroslaw Haymanowych from the Rosemount parish in Montreal.[340] Rev. Haymanowych served the parish in Val-D'Or and in Rouyn in 1965-66.[341] In 1966, Rev. Chayka returned to Val-d'Or and Rev. Haymanowych returned to Montreal. In 1967, the Ukrainian Catholic Church finally made the last payment on its mortgage to the local branch of the Canadian Imperial Bank of Commerce.[342] The Church remains as a permanent monument to the Ukrainian presence in Val-d'Or.

In January, 1967, the UNF Choir, Dnipro, from Sudbury performed in Val-d'Or as part of the annual Ukrainian New Year and Independence Day celebrations.[343] The celebration of the Canadian Centennial in 1967 and the Montreal Expo attracted a number of former Val-d'Or residents to Montreal. A few made a special trip in the summer months to visit Val-d'Or and the remaining members of the Ukrainian community.

In 1968, the towns of Val d'Or and Bourlamaque[344] were amalgamated for form a new town but with the name of Val-d'Or. In the 1971 census, there were 160 Ukrainians in Val-d'Or in a total population of 17,421. There were 35 Ukrainians in Malartic and 20 in Duparquet. There was a total of 255 Ukrainians in Abitibi County.[345]

During the 1960s, some of the members of the left-wing community had the opportunity to visit Soviet Ukraine and meet their relatives. In some cases, these visits reinforced their loyalty to their political beliefs but in other cases, they were disappointed with the relatively low standard of living that was not significantly higher than when they left for Canada in the late 1920s. Upon their return, a few individual members withdrew from any further political activity. The small and aging pro-communist group continued to hold their regular fund-raising and occasional social events in private homes that were sometimes reported in their national press.

The RCMP continued periodic surveillance on the Ukrainian left-wing community. There were eleven members of the AUUC in 1967.[346]

On the 50th anniversary of the Soviet Revolution, a banquet was held on 16 November, 1968 and $212.00 was raised from 18 donors for the Canadian pro-Soviet press.[347] In 1969, the RCMP reported that the advanced age of the persons who were involved in AUUC activities and their lack of activities no longer made the local organization the subject of interest. They were no longer considered '... a threat or bear any influence within the (Ukrainian) community'.[348] In 1970, the RCMP reported that few if any people are aware of this organizations existence in Val-d'Or and no political activity was detected. In February, 1971, the RCMP decided to suspend any further reporting on the Ukrainian left-wing community in Val-d'Or.[349]

The succeeding years from 1971 to 1982 were marked by the deaths of the more prominent members of the Ukrainian left-wing community. In a few cases, older members moved to the larger urban centers of southern Ontario to be closer to family and friends.[350]

# THE DECLINE OF THE COMMUNITY

## 1967-1991

In the 1970s, the economy of the Abitibi region was beginning to slide into a rapid decline. Of the thirteen mines operating in the Val-d'Or and Malartic area in 1963, seven were open in 1971 and only four were in operation in 1979. In December, 1967, Sullivan Mine closed.[351] In November, 1971, Manitou-Barvue laid off 140 miners and planned to close in 1972. The mine continued to operate until 1978.[352] Rumours were reported that the Lamaque mine would also close.[353]

According to a local survey conducted in 1971, half of the population in Val-d'Or received income from government sources. They worked either for the various levels of government, the military or were on welfare.[354] Despite the increase in the price of gold from $42.00 per ounce in 1971 to $150.00 per ounce in 1973, the local mining economy continued to decline. In 1965, there were 2463 miners in the Val-d'Or and Malartic region and in 1976, there were only 1478.[355] In April, 1976, the Department of National Defence moved out of the Val-d'Or base that was established as an RCAF base in 1954 and the Department of Transport took over responsibility for the airport.[356] Despite the economic difficulties, the total population of Val-d'Or increased from 17,451 in 1971 to 19,915 in 1976.[357]

The UNF decreased their activities to the point that in 1965 the UNF National Executive sent their Secretary to visit the branch to discuss the situation. After 1966, there were only 9 to 13 members. The UNF hall was rented for other purposes. For many years in the 1970s no minutes were kept of UNF branch meetings.[358] The UNF branch also suffered from the death of their earliest members and also the departure of a few to other parts of Canada.[359]

There was also a decline in the numbers of the local Polish community. When the Val-d'Or branch of the Polish Canadian Mutual Aid Society celebrated its 25th anniversary in 1972, there were 34 members. There were 70 members in 1947.[360]

In 1973, a dispute arose over property taxes on the Ukrainian Catholic Church and it was reported in the local press in July that the church was sold for non-payment of taxes. It seems that Rev. Chayka had to pay the sum of $341.00 that *The Star* alleged was not paid. A special fund was organized and led by *The Star* to buy back the church. By the end of October, *The Star* reported that the recovery fund had reached its goal. Donations were received from residents of Val-d'Or and former Ukrainian residents from various parts of Canada.[361] The Ukrainian Catholic Church continued to function but with an aging parish.[362] In 1975, the problems of administering parishes with small congregations in Rouyn and Val-d'Or were well known in the larger community.[363] The parish hall was rented to a local Québécois association to pay for the on-going church expenses. The few remaining families often met in their homes to celebrate various social events and anniversaries.

The Ukrainian Catholic Church was vandalized in March, 1975.[364] Later, the building was damaged by fire on 28 October, 1976 and the damages amounted to $20,000. A bank account was opened at the Royal Bank to raise funds for repairs.[365] A concert featuring the Dnipro dance group from Ottawa was held on 5 December, 1976 to raise funds for the repair of the Church.[366]

In 1975, there were 9 members of the Val-d'Or branch of the Ukrainian Catholic Women's League: P. Sikorsky, O. Chayka, O. Chayka-Havryliuk, K. Shtalenko, M. Liakhovych, O. Hryniuk, N. Andrusyshyn, M. Styranka, M. Sakharnatska.[367]

The Quebec nationalist movement gained momentum in the 1970s and on November 15, 1976 the Parti Québécois (PQ) was elected in the Quebec provincial elections. The PQ was elected partly because of their promise to hold a referendum on 'sovereignty-association' that is, to enter into negotiations with the federal government regarding the future status of Quebec. The referendum was held on 20 May, 1980 and 60% voted against the plans to negotiate separatism. However, according to the statistical reports, 50% of the Québécois (other than Anglophones and the immigrant population) supported this option.

During 1978, Father Chayka arranged a number of celebrations, dinners and other community events that included participation from the larger Québécois community.[368] On 6 September, 1981, Rev. Chayka organized a series of events to celebrate the 50th anniversary of Ukrainians in Abitibi. The UNF Choir from Montreal performed a concert for the larger community. An episcopal Mass was also celebrated with Bishop Isidore Borecky from Toronto.[369]

On 23 February, 1982, a fire broke out in the UNF hall and it suffered fire damage. The hall was sold and the UNF branch was formally dissolved. A UNF branch financial account was maintained for memorial purposes. The hall was purchased by George Sup, a member of the Ukrainian community originally from Lac Castagnier, who rebuilt it for commercial purposes. It was still used for another ten years by the Ukrainian community for dances, weddings and various social events.

Former members of the AUUC and WBA who remained in Val-D'Or continued to send donations to the newspaper, *Zhyttia i Slovo* press fund in Toronto. The youth had nearly all moved to larger centers in southern Ontario and elsewhere returning to visit relatives on holidays and special occasions.

The small Russian Orthodox Church continued to function with Father David Shevchenko but with few parishioners.[370] He had to support this church and the Russian Orthodox Church in Rouyn-Noranda on his small pension.[371] He collapsed in church and died at the age of 92 on 16 April, 1981. He was buried in Hamilton, Ontario. There were no other permanent Russian Orthodox priests to serve the few remaining parishioners.[372] The small church remained closed except when visiting priests held religious services on special occasions. The church was permanently closed in 1982 and made into an architectural monument and local tourist attraction. Some of the icons were sent to the Russian Orthodox Chapel near La Ferme, the location of the First World War Internment Museum.

In the 1980s and 1990s, researchers became interested in the story of the internment of the Ukrainians during the First World War. As a result of detailed research, nation-wide organization and lobbying with the federal government, an interpretation centre was later established at La Ferme on the original site of the internment camp. This museum became a popular destination for tourists and also members from the Ukrainian community. Among the Directors of this museum was Marcel Kurello, a descendent of the Ukrainian pioneers in Lac Castagnier.

In 1981, out of a total population of 21,190 in Val-d'Or, those of British ancestry were 955, French Canadian ancestry were 18,790 and Ukrainian origin were 140.[373] In the Ukrainian community, there were 85 males and 45 females reflecting the continuing male predominance characteristic of mining towns. The long years of working in the mines began to have an effect on the miners. Some began to develop serious ailments that prevented them from further work or enjoying their retirement.[374] With the advance of age and related illness, some of the members of the Ukrainian community moved to southern Ontario to live with their children and also benefit from the available medical services.[375]

The opening of the James Bay hydroelectric projects and the roads linking the projects to the Abitibi area boosted the local economy. In 1983, the unemployment rate was 23% of the labour force. In January, 1985, it was announced that the Lamaque Mine would close in the spring.[376] In 1987, the unemployment rate fell to 10% due to another 'gold boom' as a result of the uncertain international economic situation. International gold prices rose to $474.00 an ounce in United States dollars in May, 1987.[377] Despite the 'boom-and-bust' evolution of the mining economy in Val-d'Or, there were signs of optimism in the late 1980s. The financial inducements by the federal government to promote prospecting had resulted in the opening of new mines in the Abitibi region and the prices of houses increased in Val-d'Or. The introduction of sophisticated mining machinery required a well-trained workforce and salaries increased.[378] In 1987, a new airport complex was completed to serve the increased traffic and the developing northern and arctic communities.[379] However, there were few members of the community who were ready and able to take advantage of the new economic opportunities. The fate of the remaining Ukrainian families was closely tied to the survival of the small Anglophone community that in many respects, acquired all the characteristics of an ethnocultural group. By March, 1990, the local English-language newspaper, *The Star* ceased publication due to limited circulation.

With the death or departure of former members of the left-wing group, a small core of elderly retired people remained in Val-d'Or.[380] They continued to send donations to the Ukrainian left-wing press in Toronto. A few individuals visited the Soviet Union in group tours and took their winter holidays in Cuba.

In July, 1985, Percival High School held a reunion for former students. The event was successful and attracted former students from across Canada. According to the list of registrants[381], there were 19 former students who were of Ukrainian origin. Their places of origin indicated the extent of the out-migration of many former students and their families:

| | |
|---|---|
| Metro Toronto | 7 |
| Val-d'Or | 4 |
| Malartic | 2 |
| Burlington | 2 |
| Pierrefonds (Que.) | 1 |
| Sault Ste. Marie | 1 |
| Sarnia | 1 |
| Hull, (Que.) | 1 |

Another reunion of both high schools, the Perci-Joe Reunion, was held in Val-d'Or in August, 1990. Other reunions were held in Toronto and informal get-togethers of former residents from Val-d'Or were held in Ottawa.

Fr. Lev Chayka continued the well-established tradition of organizing Ukrainian New Year Suppers in January of each year to which local dignitaries from the Québécois community were invited.[382] During the 1980s, this New Years Supper or Malanka was the main Ukrainian community event in Val-d'Or. For his efforts among the local Québécois community, Fr. Chayka was awarded the Laureat of Cultural Communities for the province of Quebec for 1986 along with a $15,000 cash award.[383] In 1988, the province created the Chayka Foundation with a $5,000 grant from the provincial government.[384] In January, 1988, Fr. Chayka celebrated in addition to the New Year and Ukrainian Independence Day, the Millennium of Christianity in Ukraine.[385] The Church Hall remained vacant or was rented to various individuals and organizations and over the years, this included a children's dance school. In 2017, the Hall was rented to a local Québécois cultural group interested in media production.[386] In 2002, Fr. Chayka received a grant from the Taras Shevchenko Foundation in Winnipeg to begin the planning for a Ukrainian Cultural-Historical Museum in Val-d'Or. This Museum was planned as a building next to the Ukrainian Catholic Church. He also solicited donations from across Canada for this project. However, this project never proceeded beyond the planning stage.[387]

On 4-5 August, 1990, John and Mary Smoly celebrated their 50th wedding anniversary in the old UNF hall. This was one of the last Ukrainian community events held in this hall. The anniversary was an opportunity for many former residents to return to Val-d'Or. A Ukrainian band from Toronto performed at this event bringing back memories of all the events held in the hall since the 1930s.[388] Some former residents also returned either to be married in the Ukrainian Catholic Church or have their children baptized as documented in the Appendix. Others who were born and raised in Val-d'Or, visited the area with their families during the summers and renewed acquaintances with the remaining members of the Ukrainian community, former fellow students and the larger French and English-speaking community.[389]

With the declaration of Ukrainian independence on 24 August, 1991, there was a revival of interest and activity in the small Ukrainian community. This historic event coincided with the celebrations relating to the Centennial of Ukrainian immigration to Canada. The few remaining families and individuals including the parish priest took advantage of the political changes to visit their ancestral villages in Ukraine, some making several trips to see their relatives. Now in retirement, most were able to financially assist their relatives and hope for better future for Ukraine. There were also a few individual visits from Ukraine to visit relatives in Val-d'Or. In one case, Nicholas Tomcio, who arrived as a young Displaced Person in the late 1940s to Val-d'Or, now had the opportunity to return to Ukraine on assignment as a consultant in the Ukrainian Ministry of Communications.[390] George Tuhachevsky, another former Displaced Person, who arrived in Val-d'Or as a miner in 1948 and later moved to southern Ontario, donated $350,000 to establish the new Ukrainian Embassy in Ottawa.[391]

Another significant political event was the Quebec Referendum held on 30 October, 1995 in support of Quebec separatism by the Parti Québécois (PQ). The Referendum was preceded by an emotional campaign led by the pro-federalist movement. Professional organizers including a Ukrainian fieldworker from the federal Liberal Party were sent to mobilize the ethnocultural communities to vote 'No' that is, against separatism. However, there is no evidence that the Ukrainian fieldworker visited the Abitibi region. The results were very narrow with 50.58 % voting for the 'No' option. Premier Jacques Parizeau, leader of the PQ government, blamed the loss of this Referendum on 'money and the ethnic vote' and to a large extent, he was right.

Due to his many years in Val-d'Or, Fr. Chayka remained as the 'spokesman' for the declining Ukrainian community in Abitibi. He was interviewed by Karina Osiecka, a journalist for *L'Echo Abitibien* as 'the founder of Ukrainian churches' and the interview was published on 6 September, 2013. In this interview, Fr. Chayka described his career as a parish priest in Abitibi. In addition to his pastoral duties, Fr. Chayka mentioned his radio program on CKVD that broadcasted news of community events for many years and also his work to denounce the communist regime in the Soviet Union. He noted the decline in the number of the Ukrainian population since the 1970s and also the decline in church attendance.[392] Among the families with one Ukrainian parent, most attended the Roman Catholic Churches if at all. Fr. Chayka claimed that there were still about about 125 families in the Abitibi area including Val-d'Or, Amos and Matagami. He suggested that a Ukrainian Catholic priest from Kirkland Lake, Ontario will replace him when the time came. A documentary was made by Nadine Beaudet entitled, *Le cosaque et la gitane* of both Régine Gabrysz and Rev. Leo Chayka. The documentary was released on 1 November, 2013 and as a DVD on 29 April, 2014. At that time, both were almost 90 years of age and they remembered their childhoods spent in Ukraine and the Soviet Union. The documentary described their arrival in Abitibi in the early 1950s when the Polish and Ukrainian communities were flourishing but by 2013, Fr. Chayka and Régine Gabrysz were considered as the 'last of the first' East European immigrants.

For his long record of pastoral work in Abitibi, Fr. Leo Chayka was awarded the title of Monsignor by the Ukrainian Catholic Bishop in Toronto on 17 February, 2015. A banquet and cultural performance was held in Toronto in his honour on 29 October, 2017. This was an occasion for former residents from the Abitibi region living in southern Ontario

**Ukrainian Labour Temple**, 11th street, Val-d'Or, 2008. This building, which is now a private residence, used to serve as a a meeting place for members of the local branch of the Association of United Ukrainian Canadians (AUUC). *Photo credit:* Myron Momryk

to hold a reunion and share stories about their early years in Val-d'Or, Rouyn and Kirkland Lake.

The rivalry between the nationalists and pro-communists which fuelled the community activities for so many years was now effectively over. However, the large majority of the existing community was Canadian-born and based their involvement in the community on their Canadian experiences and the extent and quality of their initiation into the community in their youth. Recent political events in Ukraine have revived some interest in Ukrainian affairs and in their Ukrainian identity.

# THE LEGACY

**The Spirit Lake Internment Camp**
By the 1980s, researchers and academics began to write about the Canadian internment operations during the First World War. Internment operations in Canada began with the outbreak of war in 1914 and ended in 1920, although the war was over by 11 November, 1918. Until the early 1980s, it is not known if anyone had any information about these internment camps in Val-d'Or. Yurij Luhovy, a professional documentary maker from Montreal, included a visit to the Spirit Lake Internment Camp in his documentary film, *'Ukrainians in Quebec 1891-1945*'*(1979)*.

There are only a few records left by former internees about their experiences in the internment camps during the First World War. If any former internees spoke about their years of internment, it was only to their families. In some cases, their children and grandchildren did not believe their stories. From the early 1980s, Ukrainian community organizations especially the Ukrainian Canadian Civil Liberties Association began a national campaign to educate the Ukrainian Canadian community and the larger Canadian population about the existence of these camps and the injustice done to the immigrants from Austro-Hungary including the Ukrainians. The Spirit Lake Camp site was visited by interested Ukrainian Canadians and memorials were erected to designate the Camp as a historic site. This campaign was successful and in 2005, the Canadian Federal Government passed the Internment of Persons of Ukrainian Origin Recognition Act and in 2008 established the Endowment Council of the Canadian First World War Internment Recognition Fund.

A local committee was created to establish an internment centre on the site of the Camp at La Ferme. Leading members of the committee were James Slobodian and Marcel Kurello. The local Roman Catholic Church at La Ferme was purchased in 2007 for a nominal sum and the interior of the Church was rebuilt as an interpretation centre. The Spirit Lake Internment Interpretive Centre was officially opened on 24

November, 2011 in a ceremony that included politicians and visitors from Ottawa, Montreal and Ukrainian and Québécois clergy. The Centre had a permanent display of artifacts and description of historical events relating to the First World War. The Centre was founded through a major grant from the First World War Internment Recognition Fund and the Taras Shevchenko Foundation, and support from the Ukrainian Canadian Congress, the Ukrainian Canadian Civil Liberties Association and many individual Ukrainian Canadians. The main purpose of this interpretation center was to educate the local population about the First World War internment operations, increase knowledge of all aspects of Canadian history and avoid similar mistakes in the future. The center was open during the summer and was visited by students from local

**Historical plaque at the site of the Spirit Lake Internment Camp** (1999).
*Photo credit:* Myron Momryk

schools, tourist and tour groups from Montreal and other centres.[393] The documentary film, *Ukrainians in Quebec, 1891-1945,* was released as a DVD in 2010 and exhibited at the Interpretive Centre for the visitors.

Although the Museum had been established, research activities continued and one project was the restoration of the Camp cemetery containing the remains of 16 individuals including children who passed away at the Spirit Lake Camp.

However, the isolated site of this interpretative centre, the long distances from major urban centres, the high cost of heating the building during the long winters, created a financial crisis and the centre was closed and the building sold in 2019.

**The Sheptetski Colony (Lac Castagnier)**
The name 'Sheptetski' continues to appear on some of the early maps of northwestern Quebec indicating the location of the original community. The settlement was 'rediscovered' by Yurij Luhovy, and he also included a visit to Lac Castagnier in his documentary film, *'Ukrainians in Quebec 1891-1945'.* In 1991, one family still farmed in the area of the original settlement.[394] A few descendants of the original Ukrainian settlers owned buildings in the area that they use as summer residences and for hunting. The land claimed by Father Josaphat Jean remained intact and it was only in 2017 that the Basilian Order realized that Father Jean had donated this land to the Order. The local cemetery is still maintained and contains several monuments with the names of the first Ukrainian pioneers. After the establishment of the Internment Museum near Amos, some informal discussions were held among descendants of the Sheptetski colony to restore the school building and perhaps create a display dedicated to Fr. Jean. However, the need for continual fund-raising for the Internment Museum interfered with this plan.

In August, 2016, the Municipality of La Morandière erected a flagpole with the Ukrainian blue-and-yellow flag next to the flag of the Municipality and the Quebec and Canadian flags in front of the City Hall. This event was in recognition of the contribution of Ukrainian settlers to the development of this region of Quebec. This Municipality is the amalgamation in 1983 of Lac Castagnier originally named Sheptetski. Marcel Kurello, a descendant of original pioneers of this settlement, was instrumental in arranging the flag event.[395] This flag-raising also marked the 125th anniversary of Ukrainian settlement in Canada and that the settlement of Ukrainians in Quebec remained a permanent legacy of the area. The intent was to ensure that the Ukrainian contribution is also documented in school texts for future generations.

In reviewing the history of the Sheptetski Colony, it is possible to arrive at some alternate conclusions regarding the reasons for its establishment in the 1920s. At that time, the Canadian federal government had a strict immigration policy that gave preference to farmers and farm workers to immigrate to Canada and claim homesteads in western Canada. Domestics and railway workers were also allowed to immigrate to Canada at that time. With the establishment of the Sheptetski Colony, it may be suggested that Ukrainian immigrants would be encouraged to settle in the colony as farmers and farm workers and then, if they chose, leave for other parts of Canada. This was one method to ensure Ukrainian immigration to Canada in the 1920s and 1930s and escape from the political and economic problems in Yugoslavia and Halychyna, then administered by Poland. After the Second World War, the Basilian Order acquired a farm near Grimsby in the Niagara Peninsula for the same purpose. The farm was intended to welcome Ukrainian Displaced Persons and their families who did not qualify for various reasons under the 'Bulk Labour Schemes' to enter Canada. There were some stories of Ukrainian Displaced Persons in

Cemetery monument,
Lac Castagnier (Sheptetski), 2008
Photo credit: Myron Momryk

this category that arrived as farm labourers sponsored by the Basilian Order, lived and worked on the farm near Grimsby and then left for other parts of Canada. Fr. Josaphat Jean died in Grimsby on 8 June, 1972.

**Val-d'Or**

Perhaps the last remaining monument to the Ukrainian presence in Val-d'Or is the Ukrainian Catholic Church. Divine Liturgies are rarely held in the Church and the Church Hall is rented to local community organizations when possible. For many years, Michael Steranka served as a Diak (Cantor) during the Divine Liturgies. However, when he was no longer physically able to perform this duty, services in the Church were generally discontinued for the remainder of the years. Unfortunately, the Church has been rarely occupied and as a result, subject to recent acts of vandalism.[396] In 2019, the Church Residence was occupied by Monsignor Chayka. Thanks to his efforts the street in front of the Church was named rue d'Ukraine to honour the Ukrainians who are considered as one of the 'fondateurs de Val-d'Or' and who contributed to the development and history of the town.[397]

Members of the Ukrainian Community on the steps of **Protection of the Blessed Virgin Mary**, Ukrainian Catholic Church, Val-d'Or, circa 1960. *Photo credit:* La Société d'histoire et de généalogie de Val-d'Or

An important legacy of the Ukrainian experience in Val-d'Or is the references to the Ukrainian community in published histories of the area. In the more recent decades, there was a growing awareness among the local Québécois community through these historical studies of the contributions made by the immigrant and ethnocultural groups to the development of the region. Among the more significant histories in French are the publications: Odette Vincent, *Histoire de l'Abitibi-Témiscamingue*, (IGRC, 1995),[398] Denys Chabot, Jean l'Homeau and Jean Robitaille, *Histoire de Val-d'Or des origins à 1995* (1995) and Denys Chabot, *Val-d'Or*, (2009). When discussing the development of Val-d'Or in historical terms, references are always made to the contributions by Ukrainians and other immigrant groups to prospecting, mine development, the mine labour population and also the cultural activities that made Val-d'Or unique in many ways. In recent years, there is a growing awareness for the need for new immigrants to the Val-d'Or region to continue the development of the mining economy and cultural life of the community. Community organizations have been established to welcome new arrivals from Montreal and new immigrants from Africa, Arab countries and as far away as Brazil. These new attitudes are in contrast to the general isolationist attitudes among the 'host' French Canadian society in the 1940s and 1950s. However, there is still some resistance among certain segments of the host population to 'foreign customs and religions' continuing aspects of traditional attitudes.

# CONCLUSION

The evolution of the Ukrainian community in Val-d'Or-Bourlamaque demonstrated how this group was shaped to a large extent by the socio-economic structure of the one-industry mining town as well as by the general historical forces that influenced the Ukrainian Canadian community as a whole. The geographical isolation of the town and the community created a situation where only the more adventurous would travel and work. The early years meant frontier conditions of life and work that attracted predominantly single males but few females. This imbalance which continued throughout the history of the community affected the quality of life in the community. The isolation of the Abitibi region from the rest of Quebec continued to be a significant factor in the development of Val-d'Or and area for many more decades.

The mining industry with its requirements for physical abilities and stamina was almost entirely male-dominated. Also shift work in the mines ensured that some segment of the community could not effectively participate in the community activities. There were few if any jobs for women except in the few service industries such as hotels and restaurants. This created and perpetuated a situation where young girls upon completion of the local high school were obliged to seek employment in the larger urban centers. This was also the case of many young men who did not see a future in the mining industry.

However, it should be mentioned that there were individual cases of Ukrainian students from Val-d'Or studying at the mining school in Haileybury, Ontario. Also, the general working conditions in the mines encouraged those with higher education and therefore with some measure of choice to leave for larger urban centers for better employment. New arrivals from Europe or from other parts of Canada with post-secondary education had difficulty in finding interesting positions other than those in the local mining industry and soon left.

This situation deprived the community of a variety of skilled professionals and specialists who were potential role models and community leaders. High mobility and turnover created and maintained a sense of a transitory community.[399] Also the departure of many of the younger members deprived the community of successor generations. Clubs and organizations had to be continually founded and re-established to reflect the turnover in membership and cope with the lack of continuity. With the decreasing number of Ukrainians in the community, many local issues within the surviving organizations became personalized and sometimes resulted in bitter personal disputes. These conflicts further fragmented the small community and impaired social and cultural activities.

As in most one-industry towns, the local social structure reflected the hierarchical structure in the mining industry. In a small community such as Val-d'Or, the distribution of jobs was very visible and the Ukrainians and other ethnocultural groups were acutely conscious of their place in the job structure. Although there were many exceptions, a standard perception developed among the larger community and within the Ukrainian community regarding the place of each group within the local social structure. The managers and skilled workers were largely Anglophones, bilingual Francophones assumed positions in middle management and the ordinary miners were Québécois and those of European descent.

The identification of all Ukrainians in the larger community as 'miners' created a stereotype that endured in the popular imagination. The linking of an ethnocultural group with an occupational category was an unfortunate situation with potential political complications. This perception of the local social structure endured for many years and began to change only in the mid-1970s with the election of a Parti Québécois government in Quebec. The Anglophone managers and professionals were gradually replaced by French-speaking Québécois.

However, the social structure and population demographics enabled the Ukrainian and other ethnocultural groups to maintain their local identity for a relatively longer time under difficult social and economic circumstances. The total number of the local English Canadian population was not substantially larger than the European-origin population.[400]

A large percentage of the Anglophones especially those attending the English-Catholic school system were in fact bilingual Québécois. The European-origin population was not subject to the same formal and informal pressures of an overwhelming and dominating Anglophone society to integrate and assimilate as in the large urban centers. The lack of a 'critical mass' as found in the larger urban centres delayed the assimilation of the immigrants and their descendants. Almost all Ukrainian students attended the English-language schools and the larger Québécois society did not have any organizations specifically directed at welcoming and integrating the European immigrants and their descendants. The population of European origin including the Ukrainian immigrants and their families, was able to develop and maintain their own variant of their culture and identity in Val-d'Or. This local variant was related to the larger Ukrainian Canadian identity but unique in many ways to northern Ontario and Quebec.

The opening of the mines in the mid-1930s following the cessation of any significant immigration to Canada after 1931, created an age cohort that aged as a group without much reinforcement from younger and more recent Ukrainian immigrants. The arrival of the Displaced Persons after the Second World War and the cessation of any further immigration after 1952 created another age cohort that aged together as a group. The second and third waves of Ukrainian immigration arrived in Canada during periods of economic prosperity (1924-30 and 1947-52). A significant percentage was able to establish themselves during their first years in Canada and start families.

Their period of founding families was limited according to their age (usually younger years) and also according to their economic circumstances. The children born during these early immigrant years also formed age cohorts depending on the wave of immigration and the economic circumstances. An age cohort of children was formed during the years 1924-30 with another cohort during the early 1940s when the Depression ended and the economy revived with the outbreak of the Second World War. A third age cohort was formed with the 'baby-boom' generation with the highest numbers born during the years 1946-52. This situation greatly affected the life of the community because it enforced an artificial life-cycle of community activities that corresponded to the age groups of its members.

As the members became older, fewer new activities were undertaken and all efforts were concentrated on preserving the existing annual cycle of social and political events that inevitably decreased in number. A large 'gap' developed between the age cohorts, that is, the miners and their children which effectively reduced and prevented any sense of organizational and community continuity.[401]

In the small community, active and influential members were required to provide much needed leadership. The level of community activity reflected the involvement of the few hard-working members. The arrival of national organizers or community leaders with organizing skills dramatically raised the levels of activity and participation. But once they left or withdrew from the community, the level of activity dropped accordingly. This phenomenon was characteristic of the history of the Ukrainian community in Val-d'Or.

The political differences between the nationalists and communists had a profound impact on the development of the community. The fundamental political differences were also stimulated by the economic conditions encountered by the second and third waves of immigration. The second wave of immigration was severely marked by their experiences during the Depression of the 1930s. Many were encouraged to immigrate to Canada by agents of railway companies with promises of land and work opportunities. However, when the Depression began in October, 1929, these recent immigrants became economic outcasts and as individuals and as a community suffered the consequences. The Depression affected both the nationalist and communist communities and influenced their attitudes and relationship with the third wave of immigration that arrived after the Second World War. The third wave of immigration arrived in a period of relative prosperity and this economic climate encouraged an attitude of optimism and growth among the more recent arrivals that distinguished them from the earlier waves of immigration. This question of attitudes and approaches to life in Canada formed a profound division between the two waves of immigration.

The pro-communist segment rooted in the second wave of immigration and devastated by their experiences during the Depression, following their political philosophy sought to broaden their community by cooperating with other ethnocultural groups with the same political orientation according to 'class lines'. The nationalist segment sought to build their own community structures but also formed formal and informal alliances with other anti-communist groups. These alliances often took the form of personal friendships with local French Canadian politicians, religious and community leaders. Both segments of the community lived as two solitudes avoiding each other when possible.

The predominance of males and the small numbers meant a limited selection of marriage partners from within the same ethnocultural community. This situation was especially difficult for the members of the pro-communist group that had to seek partners from among the fellow left-wing ethnocultural groups or the local Québécois and Anglophone population. Many of the young miners who arrived to work in the early years left for the larger centers for these reasons. In a few cases, partners were sought in the larger centers and then persuaded to settle and live in Val-d'Or.

The Ukrainian community members who were part of the second wave of Ukrainian immigration to Canada (1924-39), shared as their common historical and political experiences the events surrounding the First World War, the East European Revolution, the Polish occupation, emigration to Canada, the Depression and the Second World War. These experiences were an integral part of their national identity and their individual identity as Ukrainians in Val-d'Or. The third wave of immigration (1947-52) shared the experiences of the Second World War in Ukraine, forced labour in Germany, the Displaced Persons Camps and immigration to Canada.

The Canadian-born and 'baby boom' generation knew only their own experiences of growing up in the Ukrainian community in Val-d'Or. Their ethnocultural and individual identity was shaped by their awareness of the collective experiences of their parents and their own participation in the various Ukrainian community events. This identity was defined and reinforced in direct relationship to their involvement in the community. Some attended the SUM (CYM) School and were introduced to the basics of community politics at that time. However, in all cases, their common point of reference was their formative years in Val-d'Or which was a totally Canadian experience and their Ukrainian identity was therefore an important part of their Canadian - and some may add Québécois - identity.

The rise of Québécois nationalism in the 1960s was also felt in Val-d'Or. Some of the local French Canadian students, studying in Montreal, returned home and brought the opinions and attitudes sympathetic to Quebec separatism and independence. In the early 1960s, the slogan 'Québéc Libre' was painted on an outside wall at the St. Joseph High School in Bourlamaque. This attitude was received with some confusion in the Ukrainian community. According to some of the Ukrainian community leaders, the French Canadians had all the institutions that constituted an independent nation – French-language provincial parliament, universities, schools, banks, radio and television, social and cultural organizations. When comparing to the situation of Ukrainians in Soviet Ukraine, the Ukrainians could only dream of having only a portion of provincial political and cultural institutions and autonomy that the French Canadians enjoyed and took for granted at that time. Few, if any, Ukrainians in Val-d'Or were sympathetic to the Quebec independence movement.

Although the organized community made extensive efforts to build and maintain a Ukrainian identity within the context of the larger Val-d'Or community, the Canadian economic forces which were the underlying reasons which brought them to Val-d'Or essentially influenced the pattern of the remainder of their lives as they did the lives of all Canadians. The departure of the younger generations for the larger industrial and urban centres is characteristic of most Canadian regions. Their ethnocultural background did influence to a certain extent their choice of destination however this issue can be described as peripheral rather than central to their concerns. By becoming completely integrated into the Canadian economy, the Ukrainian immigrants and their descendants became 'Canadianized'. Those who chose to remain in Val-d'Or were few in number and by selecting spouses from the local community, became fully integrated into the local society.[402]

The 'boom and bust' cycles of the mining industry and the political and generational differences marked the evolution of the Ukrainian community in Val-d'Or. In the 'boom' or prosperous years, there was general optimism as the community grew. In the 'bust' or recession years, the community was generally pessimistic and this mood was reflected in the community activities. The internal divisions weakened the numerical strength of the community however the political differences provided the 'motor' that motivated many of their community activities. The long tradition of community activities and events have created a distinct history and identity which is uniquely Ukrainian Canadian and will no doubt endure. And this history is also an integral part of Canadian history.

# APPENDIX

Statistics of Baptisms, Marriages and Death in the Ukrainian Catholic Parish based on information held at La Société d'histoire et de généalogie de Val-d'Or.

| Years | Baptisms | Marriages | Deaths |
| --- | --- | --- | --- |
| 1945-1950 | 20 | 0 | 2 |
| 1951-1955 | 28 | 4 | 5 |
| 1956-1960 | 11 | 7 | 8 |
| 1961-1965 | 8 | 1 | 11 |
| 1966-1970 | 5 | 11 | 8 |
| 1971-1975 | 1 | 8 | 6 |
| 1976-1980 | 7 | 0 | 8 |
| 1981-1985 | 6 | 5 | 6 |
| 1986-1990 | 2 | 2 | 7 |
| 1991-1995 | 3 | 0 | 6 |
| 1996-2000 | 0 | 0 | 5 |
| 2001-2005 | 1 | 0 | 3 |

The information includes Perron and Malartic.

**Protection of the Blessed Virgin Mary,**
Ukrainian Catholic Church
on Rue de l'Ukraine, Val-d'Or, 2008.
*Photo credit:* Myron Momryk

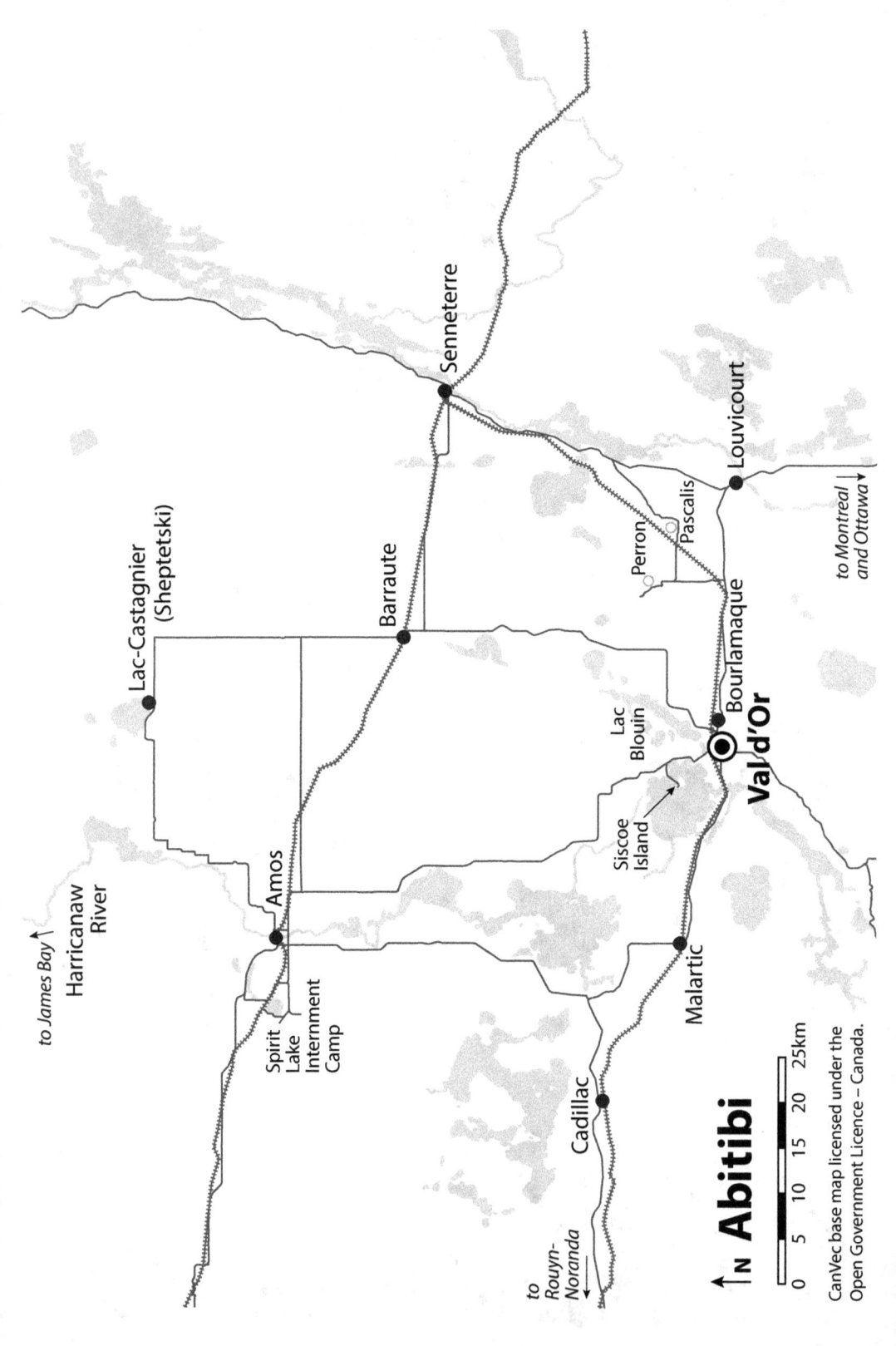

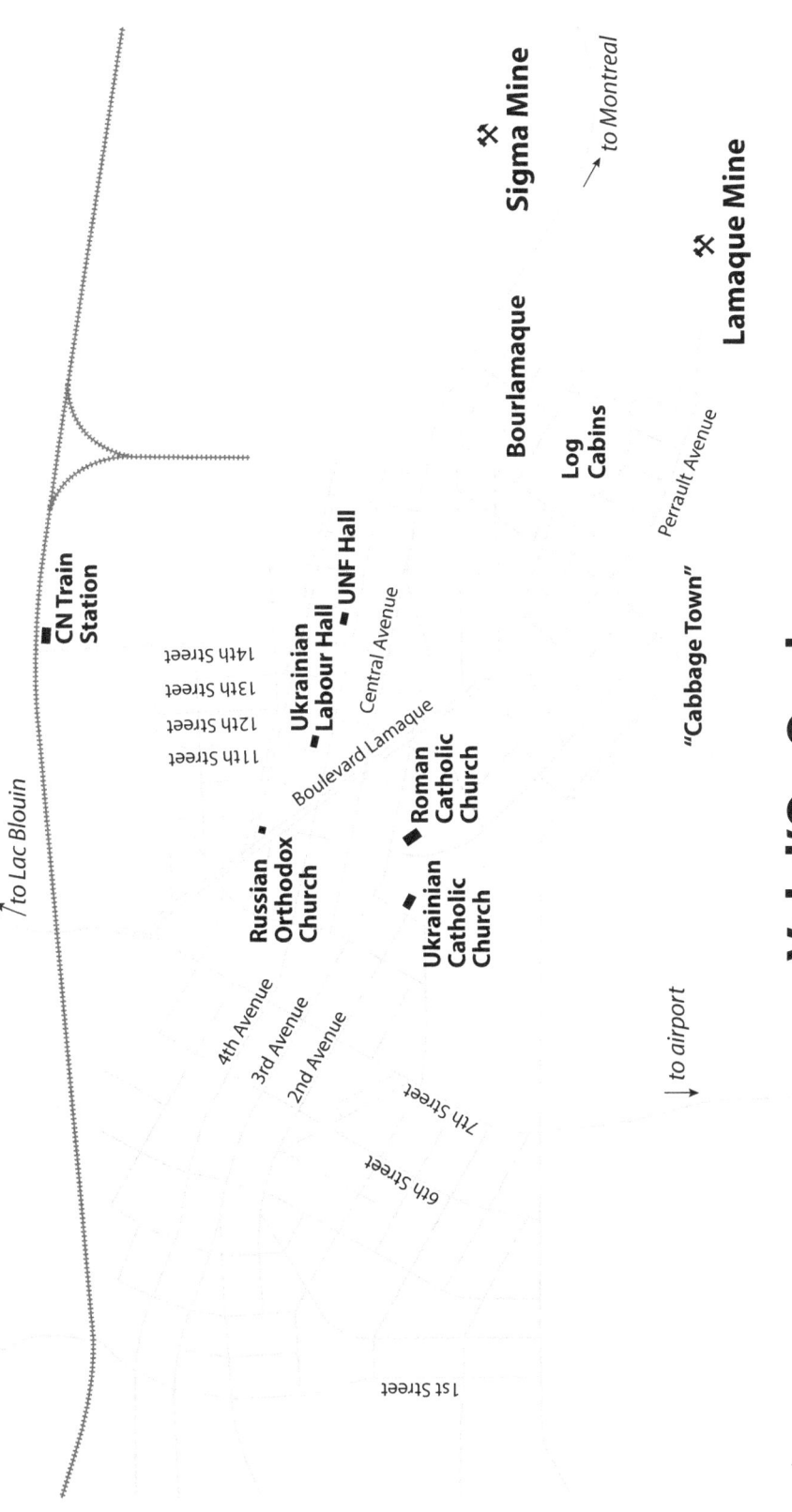

## Endnotes

1. For recent scholarship on RCMP methods of surveillance of political and social groups in Canada, see Christabelle Sethna and Steve Hewitt, *Just Watch Us, RCMP Surveillance of the Women's Liberation Movement in Cold War Canada,* McGill-Queen's University Press, Montreal and Kingston, 2018.
2. A local history entitled, *Perron Pascalis* was published by the Société d'histoire de Val-d'Or, (1996) and includes a few references with photographs to Ukrainians living in this mining town.
3. The evolution of French Canadian or Québécois perceptions of the 'ethnic question' is described in the study by Danielle Juteau, The Sociology of Ethnic Relations in Quebec: History and Discourse, *Lectures and Papers in Ethnicity* No.2, January, 1991, Robert F. Harney Professorship and Program in Ethnic, Immigration and Pluralism Studies, Department of Sociology, University of Toronto.
4. The designation 'Ukrainian' was introduced for official purposes for the first time only in the 1921 Canadian Census although some immigrants continued to identify themselves by their earlier designations.
5. Perhaps the best historical description and analysis of the first wave of Ukrainian immigration to Canada is in the publication by Orest Martynowych, *Ukrainians in Canada, The Formative Period, 1891-1924,* Canadian Institute of Ukrainian Studies Press, University of Alberta, Edmonton, 1991.
6. The research for this local history was inspired by the study by Rex A. Lucas, *Minetown, Milltown, Railtown, Life in Canadian Communities of Single Industry,* University of Toronto Press, Toronto, 1971.
7. The influence of the geology on the economy of the area is discussed in the study by Marcien Villemure, *Les Villes de la Faille de Cadillac,* Conseil Economique du Nord-Ouest Québécois, Rouyn, 1971. For information on the exploration and settlement of Abitibi-Témiscamingue, see Odette Vincent, *Histoire de l'Abitibi-Témiscamingue,* IGRC, 1995. References to the Ukrainian community are found on pages 330, 383, 395, 530.
8. Jean Laflamme, *Les Camps de Détention au Québec durant la Premiere guerre mondiale,* Montreal, 1973; Daniel Maceluch, How Ukrainians were exiled to Quebec gulag, *The Gazette,* 11 May, 1985; and also, Peter Melnycky, Badly Treated in Every Way: The Internment of Ukrainians in Quebec During the First World War in Alexander Biega and Myroslaw Diakowsky (eds.), *The Ukrainian Experience in Quebec,* The Basilian Press, Toronto, 1994, p. 51-78.

9. There is, however, a small cemetery near the former camp where a number of inmates and members of their families were buried but there is no identification or headstones. Iwan Gregoraszcruk (Hryhoraschuk) was buried in this camp cemetery. Some of the children who died while at Spirit Lake are buried in the Amos municipal cemetery.
10. Probably the last survivor of the camp was Mary Haskett whose story appeared in the *Globe and Mail* of 27 March, 1993 in the article, Waiting and Hoping for Redress.
11. The documentary film, Jajo's Secret (2009) by James Motluk is a story about such a case.
12. For an introduction to the history of the Ukrainian political left in Quebec see Yarema Gregory Kelebay, *The Ideological and Intellectual Baggage of Three Fragments of Ukrainian Immigrants: A Contribution to the History of Ukrainians in Quebec (1910-1960)*, Ph.D Concordia University, 1992, p. 67-87.
13. Myron Momryk, Zaokhochuvalni zaklyky do ukraintsiv pereseliatysia v Kanadu, (Advertisements for Ukrainian Immigrants to Canada), *Pamiatky, Arkheohrafichnyi Shchorichnyk,* Tom 7, 2007 (p. 41-44) Kyiv, Ukraine.
14. *La Gazette du Nord*, 24 December, 1926, 21 January, 1927, 2 March, 12 November, 1928.
    According to a list prepared by Mrs. Natalie Andrushyshyn in September, 1982, the colony was founded by the following individuals with their families: Matvii Borshchevsky, Pylyp Andrushyshyn, Dmytro Sup, Vasyl Mokrii, Vasyl Ostashevsky, Ivan Novosad, Arseniuk, Sylvester Lukashuk, Denys Leshchuk, Mykola Kurylo, Mykhailo Gonta, Teodor Kurylo, Mykola Lesyk, Mykhailo Hilchuk, Petro Mychka, Pavlo Kosar, Teodor Boyko, Teodor Antoniuk, Klym Karpach, Hryhorii Storozhuk, Andrii Kushnir, Antin Kokhon.
15. LAC, RG2 Series I, Order-in-Council number 1232, 25 June, 1927.
16. *Montreal Gazette,* 13 October, 1927.
17. Yarema Gregory Kelebay, *The Ideological and Intellectual Baggage of Three Fragments of Ukrainian Immigrants: A Contribution to the History of Ukrainians in Quebec (1910-1960),* PhD Concordia University, 1992, p.131-136.
18. *La Gazette du Nord*, 12 November, 1928, 9 August, 1929.
19. For a biography of Father Jean's interesting life see, Zonia Keywan, *A Turbulent Life: Biography of Josaphat Jean OSBM, 1885-1972*, Clio Editions, Montreal, 1990; also, Arthur Prevost, *Par La Croix et La Charrue*, Editions Princeps, Montréal, 1939, p.68-69.
20. *La Gazette du Nord,* 22 décembre, 1933.
21. William Darcovich (ed.), *A Statistical Compendium on the Ukrainians in Canada, 1891-1976*, University of Ottawa Press, Ottawa, 1980, p.70; See Appendix 1.

22. Information provided by Mr. Morris Lach. Also Yarema Gregory Kelebay, *The Ideological and Intellectual Baggage of Three Fragments of Ukrainian Immigrants: A Contribution to the History of Ukrainians in Quebec (1910-1960)*, PhD Concordia University, 1992, p. 127-128.
23. *Bottin Abitibi-Temiscamingue Directory*, 1935, Rouyn, p. 229.
    The following individuals were identified by Mrs. Natalie Andrushyshyn as living or owning land in Sheptetski in 1934:
    Andruszczyszyn, Philippe / Antoniuk, Fedor / Bojko, Fedor / Borschewski, Mat. / Borschewski, Mrs. Justine / Favel, Jean / Gonta, Harry / Holub, Ste. / Jean, Rev. Joseph / Kosar, Paul / Kurylo, Nic. / Lacachuk, Sylvester / Lesyh, Wazil / N. Lesyh, Nic / N. Mokry, Wasyl / Penar, Albert / Sescyszyn, Mme.B. / Seszuk, Denis / Soltis, Georges / Sup, Dimitri / Sup, Isidore / Sup, Petro / Sup, Stach / Walson, J.
24. *La Gazette du Nord*, 8 May, 1939; See also Jaroslaw Rozumnyj, (editor), The saga of Pylyp Andrusyshyn, (1896-1976) in *New Soil - Old Roots, The Ukrainian Experience in Canada*, Ukrainian Academy of Arts and Sciences in Canada, Winnipeg, 1983.
25. List of settlers who claimed land in Lac Castagnier:

    | | | |
    |---|---|---|
    | Andruszczyszyn, P. | 100 acres | 21 February, 1936 |
    | Dlugopolski, Jean | 79 acres | 30 March, 1942 |
    | Jean, Josaphat (Rev.) | 6 acres | 18 March, 1929 |
    | Kurylo, Myroslaw | 96 acres | 18 April, 1955 |
    | Hilchuk, Mike | 100 acres | 1 December, 1958 |
    | Lesyk, Nick | 94 acres | 20 October, 1948 |
    | Lukashuk, Silvester | 100 acres | 25 May, 1945 |
    | Mychka, Peter | 100 acres | 9 August, 1949 |
    | Olender, John | 94 acres | 4 June, 1949 |
    | Storozuk, Harry | 99 acres | 24 July, 1939 |
    | Sup, D. | 98 acres | 19 June, 1941 |

    ANQ (Quebec); Lettres patentes de terres, Post-Confédération, Canton: Lamorandiere, Cote: M-015.
    The Andrushyshyn family moved to Val-d'Or after the Second World War to provide better educational opportunities for their children; the Sup family moved to Val-d'Or for the same reason in the early 1960s.
26. Zonia Keywan, *Sheptytsky: A Ukrainian Settlement in Abitibi*, The Father Josaphat Jean Foundation, http://www.fatherjeanfoundation.org/settlement
27. Obituary of Michael Matthews, *The Oshawa Times*, 26 August, 1965.
28. The reason for this claim that John Matthews was born in Blind River, Ontario remains a mystery. Several requests to obtain a copy of his passport application were not successful.
29. The Northern Miner, 9 April, 23 July, 30 July, 1931; La Gazette du Nord,

26 May, 1933; Denys Chabot, Jean l'Houmeau et Jean Robitaille, *Perron Pascalis,* Société d'histoire de Val-d'Or, 1996.
30. LAC, Passenger lists; SS Empress of Australia, From Antwerp, August 18, 1934, arriving at Quebec on 27 August, 1934. Returning to Canada, John Matthews, Born Blind River, Ontario, age 46, Funds: $60,000. Passport issued in Ottawa on 29 August, 1933. Stephanie Matthews, age 31, born Stanislawow, Poland (now Ivano-Frankivsk, Ukraine).
31. Obituary: *The Globe and Mail,* 24 July, 1957. This information was provided by his daughter.
32. Laurel Sefton MacDowell, *Remember Kirkland Lake, The Gold Miners' Strike of 1941-42,* University of Toronto Press, Toronto, 1983, p.40.
33. For further information on this aspect of the Canadian mining industry see, Hugh G.J. Aitken, *American Capital and Canadian Resources,* Harvard University Press, Cambridge, 1961; also, E. S. Moore, *American Influence in Canadian Mining,* The University of Toronto Press, Toronto, 1941.
34. *Canadian Mines From the Air,* Airmaps Limited, Toronto, 1937, p. 39. For an anecdotal description of personalities and events in Val d'Or from the early years, see John Marshall, *Gold,* Lugus Publications, 1994.
35. Almost all the Ukrainians who immigrated to Canada in the years 1920-1939 arrived with Polish Passports. As a result, their Ukrainian names were spelled in the Polish alphabet and many kept this spelling of their names until their death in Canada. A few Ukrainians that lived and studied in Czechoslovakia, held Czechoslovak passports.
36. For a short history of the left-right split in another Ukrainian one-industry community, see the article by Mary Stefura entitled, The Process of Identity: A Historical Look at Ukrainians in the Sudbury Area Community, in *Laurentian University Review,* Vol. XV, No.1, November, 1982, p. 55-64.
37. Some of the first Ukrainian miners in the region found work at the Siscoe Mine; J. Polowy, M. Chwaluk, W. Primak, John Smoly. (*Bottin Abitibi-Temiscamingue Directory,* Rouyn, 1935, p.116-117).
38. *The Val D'Or Star,* 3 August, 1983, History of Bourlamaque.
39. For a recent history of Bourlamaque, see Paul Trepanier, *Living in Bourlamaque, Memory and Heritage Site of the Bourlamaque Mining Village Historical House,* Corporation du Village-Minier-de-Bourlamaque, 2015 and Camille Adam (et al.), *Gold in Our Veins, Historic site of the Old Lamaque Mine,* Corporation du Village-Minier-de-Bourlamaque, 2013. Both publications were published in bilingual format. An interesting description of life in pioneer Val d'Or was written by Leslie Roberts, Valley of Gold, *Maclean's Magazine,* 1 December, 1934.
40. *La Gazette du Nord,* 9 October, 1936.
41. LAC, Photograph of Dead Child (Ukrainian) Val d'Or 1935, William Gallaway Collection; Acc. 1968-94.

42. Obituary: Dr. Jerry Roman Zownir, *The Globe and Mail*, 10 February, 2018; Information provided by Sally Smoly who is a cousin of Dr. Zownir.
43. This was a pattern that was repeated earlier in Rouyn-Noranda. See Nicole Berthiaume, *Rouyn-Noranda, Le Développement d'une Agglomération Miniere au Coeur de l'Abitibi-Témiscamingue*, College du Nord-Ouest, Rouyn, 1981, p.24.
44. UNYF Historical Research Project, Interview with Ivan Michael Lenyk, 23 June, 1982 (Interview by Taras Pidzamecky). Obituary of Ivan Lenyk: *The New Pathway*, 23 January, 1993.
45. *Val D'Or, 1979*, Chaumont, Anjou, 1979, p.13.
46. *La Gazette du Nord*, 9 October, 1936
47. *La Gazette du Nord*, 20 November, 1936
48. *Ukrainski Robitnychi Visti*, 14 April, 1936.
    Among the early donors were: A. Romaniuk, M. Ferbiak, M. Shpak, P. Moskal, M. Karlashchuk, F. Verenich, M. Hotsyliak, P. Kyvyryha, N. Heliash, N. Aleksander, A. Makar, T. Sitko, V. Cholkan, H. Harych, I. Shapel, E. Kochman, M. Tomchak, V. Bilii, S. Ostapiv, I. Pysh, A. Horban, P. Mandryk, V. Bronitsky, N. Pelesh, I. Shkbarok (*Ukrainski Robitnychi Visti*, 8 April, 8 June, 8 December, 1936, 9 January, 10 May, 1937)
49. Joseph Duguay, L'Abitibi quand on l'habite, *Le Bulletin des Agriculteurs*, Octobre, 1942, p. 39-40.
50. See biographical note on Herman Saviuk, (Introduction) *Kalendar Slovo*, Toronto, 1977; in the *Bottin Abitibi-Témiscamingue Directory, 1935*, (Rouyn), the following Ukrainian names have been identified as involved in business in the section on Val D'Or on pages 131-136: Mike Korneluke, shoemaker; N.E. Sawka, bowling; Herman Sawiuk, restaurant; Mrs. Ustina Stchur, bowling.
51. See obituary in *The Star*, 27 January, 1982; Mike Sorokowski died on 18 January, 1982 and the funeral was held at the Ukrainian Catholic Church.
52. *Ukrainski Robitnychi Visti*, 14 May, 1936.
53. *Ukrainski Robitnychi Visti*, 29 November, 1935.
54. Archives of Ontario, Ukrainian National Federation Collection, Val d'Or Branch, Records 1936-37; also Zynovy Knysh (ed.), *Toward National Unity, Fifty Years of Service by the Ukrainian National Federation 1932-1982, Historical Almanac*, Volume I, Part 2, Toronto, 1982, p.10; The first members were: Mykhailo Danyliuk, Mykola Dovhan, Dmytro Lopukh, Mykhailo Lopukh, Matvii Mazuryk, Petro Panasiuk, Hryhir Rusnak, Sifiia Rusnak, Volodymyr Saviuk, Mykola Syrko, Mykhailo Silvashyn, Stepan Tverdun, Teodor Kuchak, Oleksa Hnatiuk, Mykhailo Stasyshyn.
55. Entry on the Ukrainian National Federation in the *Encyclopedia of Ukraine*, Volume V, St-Z, University of Toronto Press, Toronto,1993.
56. For a brief history of this parish, see the booklet by Mme Annette Gauth-

ier entitled, *Genese de nos paroisses régionales (Nord Ouest Québécois et est Ontarien)* Rouyn, 1972.
57. *Ukrainski Robitnychi Visti*, 23 June, 1936.
58. Zynovy Knysh, (ed.), *Toward National Unity*, op. cit., p. 11.
59. Among the early donors were: A. Romaniuk, M. Ferbiak, M. Shpak, P. Moskal, M. Karlashchuk, F. Verenich, M. Hotsyliak, P. Kyvyryha, N. Heliash, N. Aleksander, A. Makar, T. Sitko, V. Cholkan, H. Harych, I. Shapel, E. Kochman, M. Tomchak, V. Bilii, S. Ostapiv, I. Pysh, A. Horban, P. Mandryk, V. Bronitsky, N. Pelesh, I. Shkbarok (*Ukrainski Robitnychi Visti*, 8 April, 8 June, 8 December, 1936, 9 January, 10 May, 1937)
60. *Ukrainski Robitnychi Visti*, 4 November, 1936.
61. *Ukrainski Robitnychi Visti*, 31 October, 1936.
62. *Canadian Farmer*, 11 November, 1936.
63. Interview with Mr. Lenyk at his home in Toronto; Lenyk's store and the hall became centers of Ukrainian community life in Val-d'Or. He moved to Toronto in 1947 where he became one of the builders of the St. Demetrius Ukrainian Orthodox Church. (See obituary, *Toronto Star*, 27 December, 1992).
64. Entry for Evhen Konovalets, *Encyclopedia of Ukraine*, Volume II, G-K, University of Toronto Press, Toronto, 1988, p.599.
65. *U Pershi Rokovyny 1938-39*, Saskatoon, Saskatchewan, 1939, p. 67-68. For A list of donors from Val-d'Or; also Zynovy Knysh, (ed.), *Toward National Unity*, op. cit., p.12-20.
66. ibid.,
67. For a history of this branch, see Mary Smoly, Viddil OUK u Val d'Or in Irene Knysh (Ed.), *In Service of Our Homeland, The Ukrainian Women's Organization of Canada - 25th Anniversary (1930-1955)*, Winnipeg, n.d., p. 202-207.
68. Library and Archives Canada (LAC), Ukrainian National Youth Federation of Canada Collection, MG28 V8, Vol.10, File: Correspondence with Branches; Val d'Or, Quebec, 1939-44. The first members were: Ivan Lenyk, Olha Polova, Marusia Sup, Anna Macherniuk, Anna Mychka, Marusia Hrushchyn, Onnelia Baranovska, Myron Shan, Vasyl Shpin, Mykola Bychok, Vasyl Bizhyk, Haiduk.
69. Obituary: Frank (Fedor) Moskal (1903-1970), *Zhyttia i Slovo*, 8 February, 1971.
70. Ukrainian Dreams: www.ukrainian-dreams.com/localPeople-Mudry.php
71. Archives of Ontario, Ukrainian National Federation Collection, Val d'Or Branch, Records 1936-37; also Zenovy Knysh (ed.), *Toward National Unity*, op.cit., p. 21-22.
72. *Ukrainski Robitnychi Visti*, 23 June, 1937.
73. For further information, see Myron Momryk, Ukrainian Volunteers from

Canada in the International Brigades, Spain, 1936-39: A Profile, *Journal of Ukrainian Studies*, 16, No.1-2, (Summer-Winter 1991). The following volunteers in the International Brigades, Spanish Civil War, gave their place of origin in Canada as Val-d'Or and area or were identified as having some connection with the area. It should be emphasized that their stay in Val-d'Or could not have been more than a year or two. The volunteers also listed other places to indicate that they had travelled across Canada searching for work.

The volunteers were:
Ignatz Derkach; killed in action (also from Timmins)
Mykola Haleta
Pawel Harasimchuk (Harasimiuk)
Steve Harrost; prisoner of war
Maksym Kolbasko
Mykhailo Romaniuk
Andrei Sich; reported killed in action
Ivan Yacemec
Izyder Nagorny (may be Polish- from Siscoe)
Semen Dobrovolsky; prisoner of war
Peter Sternichuk (Starnynchuk)
John Lukasevich; killed in action (also from Rouyn)

74. *Ukrainski Robitnychi Visti*, 5 July and 8 July, 1937
75. *BC Workers News*, January 22, 1937.
76. *Narodna Hazeta*, 30 April, 1938.
77. *The Daily Clarion*, 27 January, 1938; John Kolasky, *The Shattered Illusion, The History of Ukrainian Pro-Communist Organizations in Canada*, PMA, Toronto, 1979, p.23.
78. *Narodna Hazeta*, 30 April, 1938; From these reports, it can be assumed that the Quebec Provincial Police (QPP) conducted a surveillance of the left-wing community in Val-d'Or. Whether the QPP cooperated with the RCMP in this activity cannot be confirmed. According to present information, QPP records regarding these activities are not available to researchers.
79. *Narodna Hazeta*, 13 August, 1938.
80. *Party Builder*, April, 1938.
81. *Narodna Hazeta*, 5 September, 1938.
82. *Narodna Hazeta*, 31 October, 1938 and 9 January, 1939.
83. *The Daily Clarion*, 15 November, 1938.
84. *Narodna Hazeta*, 10 September and 28 September, 1938.
85. *Narodna Hazeta*, 29 October, 1938.
86. *Narodna Hazeta*, 9 December, 1938.
87. *Narodna Hazeta*, 1 April, 1938.

88. Quebec, Department of Mines and Fisheries, *Mining Industry and Statistics, 1937,* (Quebec), 1938, p.16.
89. *Narodna Hazeta,* 16 March and 25 March, 1939.
90. Reported in the Croatian-language newspaper, *Slobodna Misao,* 18 April, 1939.
91. *Narodna Hazeta,* 10 June, 1939.
92. Laurel Sefton MacDowell, *Remember Kirkland Lake, The Gold Miners Strike of 1941-42,* University of Toronto Press, Toronto, 1983, p. 40.
93. Laurel Sefton MacDowell, *ibid.,* p.41.
94. Laurel Sefton MacDowell, *ibid.,* p.61-62.
95. Edward Peter Maruska (1918-2002) served in the Royal Canadian Air Force. Peter Wolanek enrolled in 1942 and served overseas. He was wounded three times and when he was discharged in 1945, he returned to Val-d'Or.
96. *Narodna Hazeta,* 27 November, 1939.
97. *Narodna Hazeta,* 16 January, 1939; see also, Benoit-Beaudry Gourd, Mines et Syndicats en Abitibi-Témiscaminque, 1910-1950, M.A. (History), University of Ottawa, 1978.
98. *Narodna Hazeta,* 25 January, 1940.
99. For further information, see Myron Momryk, The Royal Canadian Mounted Police and the Surveillance of the Ukrainian Community in Canada, *Journal of Ukrainian Studies,* Volume 28, No. 2, 2003; LAC, Records of the Canadian Security and Intelligence Service (CSIS), RG146, File number 93-A-00170, Association of United Ukrainian Canadians, Val d'Or-Bourlamaque, Quebec, Memorandum, 23 January, 1940; thereafter, LAC, RG146, CSIS File. A request was submitted on 18 April, 1995 under the Access to Information Act regarding any information on the Ukrainian National Federation Branch in Val-d'Or. The reply received on 17 May, 1995 from the LAC stated that no records could be located that would likely contain the information requested.
100. The First Winter War was from 30 November, 1939 to 12 March, 1940; Yrjo Raivio, *Kanadan Suomalaisten Historia* Volume II, Sudbury, 1979, p. 114; The Finnish volunteers were Eino Arppe, Vaino Autio, Walter Seppala, E. Kumpala.
101. LAC, Ukrainian National Youth Federation of Canada Collection, MG28 V8, Volume 10, File: Correspondence with Branches; Val d'Or, Quebec, 1939-44. In a letter dated 26 October, 1940, S. Huk wrote that there was hardly any youth in Val-d'Or only 3 boys and 2 girls since most had married or moved away. The UNYF (MUN) Club was essentially dormant.
102. The two miners killed were M. Peroha and Joseph Peshetulo, *Narodna Hazeta,* 31 May, 1940.
103. *Narodna Hazeta,* 6 April, 1940.

104. LAC, RG146, CSIS File, 29 April,1940.
105. LAC, RG146, CSIS File, 27 September, 1940.
106. According to the 1941 Canadian census, the language and mother tongues were:
    Slavic: Ukrainian (331); Polish (273); Russian (67); Serb-Croat (318); Slovak (187); Bulgarian (35) / Other: Finnish (202); Chinese (74)
    Racial Origin: Ukrainian (324); Russian (67); Polish (301); Czech-Slovak (153); Finnish (216)
    Religion: Greek Catholic (230); Greek Orthodox (287)
107. N.J. Hunchak, *Canadians of Ukrainian Origin, Population,* Winnipeg, 1945, p.148-149; also William Darcovich (ed.,) *A Statistical Compendium on the Ukrainians in Canada, 1891-1976,* University of Ottawa Press, Ottawa, 1980, p.70.
108. The census figures are not accurate because some Ukrainians were listed under other categories such as Polish because they held Polish passports. Also, not all Ukrainians were enumerated by the census-taker. For a short history of Duparquet, see Yves Cote, *L'Evolution et la régression d'une ville miniere, Duparquet,* Thesis L.es L., Université Laval, 1972.
    p.179, Census-Duparquet, 1941:
    Irish (116); French (643); Scots (102); Ukrainian (52); English (84); Czech and Slovak (39) / German (22)
109. LAC, RG146, CSIS File, 20 January, 1941.
110. Ibid., The Chicago restaurant was owned by Joe Lisow (Lisowsky) who immigrated to Soviet Ukraine in the 1950s.
111. *Toronto Star,* February 17, 1941
112. LAC, RG146, CSIS File, 10 April, 1941.
113. LAC, Tracy Philipps Papers, MG30 E350, Vol. 1, file 8, Letter dated 3 July, 1942 from the RCMP to Tracy Philipps. The letter continues and states that the case against Serdar was handled by the Quebec Provincial Police and was eventually disposed of on 25 February, 1942 when the case was dismissed as the evidence was contradictory. Serdar and two other miners from the region were later recruited by the British Special Operations Executive (SOE) and parachuted into Yugoslavia to establish contacts with Joseph Tito's Partisans. Serdar ended his career as a Colonel in the Yugoslav Army.
114. *Toronto Star,* July 29, 1941.
115. LAC, RG146, CSIS File, 31 July, 1941.
116. Vzaimna Pomich was a local branch of a Ukrainian pro-nationalist mutual aid (insurance) association with headquarters in Winnipeg. The equivalent pro-communist organization was the Workers' Benevolent Association.
117. *Ukrainske Zhyttia,* 24 May, 1942.
118. LAC, RG146, CSIS File, 31 July, 1941.

119. *Ukrainske Zhyttia*, 9 April and 15 July, 1942.
120. *Friends in Need, The WBA Story, A Canadian Epic in Fraternalism*, Winnipeg, Manitoba, 1972, p. 385; D.R. Peters, W. Yasko, M. Mshar were from Val D'Or.
121. Peter Krawchuk, *Our Contribution to Victory*, Kobzar, Toronto, 1985, p.78 (Photos); John Hruntey (Val-d'Or), P. Badak (Duparquet), J.P. Chomyshyn (Malartic).
122. LAC, RG146, CSIS File, 17 December, 1941.
123. LAC, RG146, CSIS File, 27 August and 5 September, 1941.
124. LAC, RG146, CSIS File, 11 September, 1941.
125. Ibid.,
126. LAC, RG146, CSIS File, 5 November and 14 November, 1941.
127. Canadian Museum of History, Archives, The Prokopchak Family fonds, File 1-27, Notebook.
128. LAC, RG146, CSIS File, 17 February, 1942
129. LAC, RG146, CSIS File, Federation of Russian Canadians in Val d'Or, Vol.1, part 3861, Request no. AH-2003/00074.
130. LAC, RG146, CSIS File, 3 July, 17 July, 6 August, 20 August, 27 August, 1942.
131. LAC, RG146, CSIS File, 4 December, 1941 (Letter).
132. LAC, RG146, CSIS File, 23 October, 1942.
133. LAC, RG146, CSIS File, 29 December, 31 December, 1942, 14 January, 4 February, 11 February, 4 March, 12 March, 25 March, 29 March, 1943
134. LAC, RG146, CSIS File, 12 March, 1943
135. LAC, RG146, CSIS File, 29 April, 1943
136. LAC, RG14, Vol.2481, File 27, 26 April, 1943.
137. LAC, RG146, CSIS File, 6, 13, 26 May, 8, 30 June, 14, 26, 27, 28 July, 12 August, 1, 16, 23 September, 12, 21 October, 1943. The activities of the Communist Party in Val-d'Or were continually reported under the captions: Communist Party of Canada, Val d'Or; Canadian Ukrainian Association, Val d'Or; and Federation of Russian Canadians, Val d'Or, P.Q.
138. LAC, RG146, CSIS File, 21 October, 1943.
139. LAC, RG146, CSIS File, 30 December, 1943, 27 January, 2 February, 15 March, 1944.
140. LAC, RG146, CSIS File, 18 February, 15 March, 1944.
141. LAC, RG146, CSIS File, 15 July, 1944.
142. LAC, RG146, CSIS File, 28 July, 1944.
143. The Labour Progressive Party was founded in 1943 because the Communist Party of Canada was still prohibited.
144. LAC, RG146, CSIS File, 27 July, 1944.
145. LAC, RG146, CSIS File, August, 1944
146. LAC, RG146, CSIS File, 27 November, 1944.

147. LAC, RG146, CSIS File, 4 January, 1945
148. LAC, RG146, CSIS File, 2 March, 1945.
149. *General Report of the Minister of Mines of the Province of Quebec for the Year Ending March 31$^{st}$, 1942,* (Quebec, 1942), p. 28.
150. See obituary of Andryi Barylo, *The New Pathway,* 20 September, 1986; Active members in 1943 were: Pavlo Koshilka, Fenia Buchok, Olia Barylo, Likeria Chvaliuk, Stepan Vynar, Mykhailo Borsuk, Iosef Kliuchkowsky, Stepan Buchok, Mykhailo Chvaliuk, Vasyl Poremsky, Ivan Lenyk (jr.).
151. LAC, Ukrainian National Youth Federation of Canada Collection, MG28 V8, Volume 10, File: Correspondence with Branches, Val d'Or, Quebec, 1939-44. At that time the members were: Slavka Lenyk, Bohdan Koshilka, Stefania Zhovnir, Zenovia Sverid, Evhenia Soia, S. Stoliarchuk, K. Olianyk, I. Sverid, A. Barylo, P. Iuskiw, S. Buchok, T. Dubek, E. Borsuk, S. Vaskan, M. Chvaliuk, G. Moroziuk, S. Vynar, O. Hnatiuk, P. Lubtsun, K. Koniukh, T. Haiduk.
152. John B. Lang, *A Lion in a Den of Daniels – History of the International Union of Mine, Mill and Smelter Workers in Sudbury, Ontario, 1942-1962,* p. 72.
153. Files on the three soldiers were obtained from the Personnel Records Centre, LAC, Ottawa. It is interesting to note that all three were listed as Roman Catholics.
154. Myron Momryk, *Remember the Flag, Mazeppa Legion History,* Montreal, 2009, p. 10.
155. LAC, Personnel Records Unit: Peter Paul Brosko was originally from Cobalt, Ontario. He worked at Sigma Mines prior to enlistment in the Royal Canadian Air Force on 11 July, 1942 and was later commissioned as a navigator/officer. He was married to Mary Kurillo from Lac Castagnier and they had a son, Peter Myroslaw, born in 1942; *Report of the No. 1 Canadian War Crimes Investigation Unit on Miscellaneous War Crimes Against Members of Canadian Armed Forces in the European Theatre of Operations, 9 September 1939 to 8 May, 1945, Part II,* p. 34.
156. Mike Koshilka, born on 29 September, 1929, and died in Collingwood, Ontario, on 9 October, 2009.
157. LAC, RG146, CSIS File, 17 May, 4 June, 1945.
158. UNYF Historical Research Project, Interview with Ivan Michael Lenyk, 23 June, 1982, (Tape two).
159. LAC, RG146, CSIS File, 17 May, 4 June, 1945.
160. LAC, RG146, CSIS File, 6 July, 1945
161. LAC, RG146, CSIS File, Letter: 2 September, 1945
162. LAC, RG146, CSIS File, 7 September, 17 October, 1945
163. LAC, RG146, CSIS File, 22 October, 1945
164. LAC, RG146, CSIS File, 12 February, 1946
165. LAC, RG146, CSIS File, 3 February, 1946

166. LAC, RG146, CSIS File, 20 April, 1946
167. LAC, RG146, CSIS File, 22 March, 29 March, 12 April, 20 April, 20 June, 16 June, 29 July, 2 August, 30 August, 1946
168. *Edinost*, 2 October, 1946.
169. LAC, RG146, CSIS File, Federation of Russian Canadians in Val d'Or, Vol.1, part 3861, Request no. AH-2003/00074, 18 March, 1949.
170. LAC, RG146, CSIS File, 26 November, 1946
171. For information on the DP immigration movement to Canada, see Myron Momryk, Ukrainian DP Immigration and Government Policy in Canada, 1946-1952, in Wsevolod W. Isajiw, Yury Boshyk and Roman Senkus (eds.), The Refugee Experience: Ukrainian Displaced Persons After World War II, CIUS Press, Edmonton, Alberta, 1992. The term 'Displaced Person' or more precisely, 'DP' was sometimes used in a derogatory fashion by Canadian-born individuals to describe the new immigrants.
172. *The Star*, 6 June, 1947.
173. Stanley Klosevych later moved to Ottawa where he became an active member of the Ukrainian community. (Interview with Stanley Klosevych)
174. There was also two deaths: Fred Zahoruk, age 89 years, who worked at the Sigma Pool Room, died on 20 April, 1945 and was buried in Noranda where he had some family. He was perhaps the oldest Ukrainian living in Val d'Or at that time. Theodore Hayduk, 41 years old, passed away on December 5, 1945 and the funeral was held at the Ukrainian UNF Hall on 10 December. John Swered, a friend, was responsible for the funeral arrangements. Val d'Or Cemetery, Box F-1 (1941-1953).
175. See obituary of Ivan Lenyk in *Novyi Shlakh* (The New Pathway), 23 January, 1993.
176. *Ottawa Evening Journal*, 3 May, 1918.
177. Peter Krawchuk, *The Ukrainian Socialist Movement in Canada, 1907-1918*, Progress Books, Toronto, 1979, p. 81.
178. In the study by Benoit-Beaudry Gourd entitled, *Mines et syndicats en Abitibi-Témiscamingue 1910-1950*, Cahiers du département d'histoire et de géographie, Rouyn, 1981, he includes a list on pages 69-70 of the mines and the number of fatal casualties for the years 1925-1949. The top ten mines and their total for fatal accidents were as follows:
Mines Total fatal casualties 1915-1949
Noranda (59); East Malartic (38); Beattie (27); Malartic Goldfields (12); Canadian Malartic (12); Waite-Amulet (12); Siscoe (10); Normetal (10); Lamaque (9); Powell-Rouyn (9)
For example, *The Star* (25 April, 2 May, 1947) reported that 11 East Malartic miners were trapped underground and later that there were 12 victims. This story also appeared in the larger daily newspapers across Canada; see *The Globe and Mail*, 25 April, 2-5 May, 1947. The main headline in the 25

April edition read, Pump Air to 11 Trapped Miners.
179. *The Globe and Mail*, 5 May, 1947; See also the article by Bryan D. Palmer and Robin Lunn entitled, The Big Sleep: The Malartic Mine Fire of 1947, in *Labour/Le Travail*, 39 (Spring, 1997) pages 225-240.
180. Walenty Storachuk, Sullivan Mine, 26 April, 1948; John Osrencak, Golden Manitou, 27 October, 1948; Walter Soltysek, Sigma Mines, 3 March, 1949; Michael Drzeznik, East Sullivan Mine, 4 March, 1950.
181. *The Val D'Or Star*, 29 July, 1949; Miners Owe Life to Polish DP's Heroism. Also, *The Globe and Mail*, 28 July, 1949, DP Hero Loses Life.
182. Sam Pavich and six friends from Malartic returning to Yugoslavia (*The Star*, 17 October, 1947). According to information in the Department of External Affairs, (LAC, RG 25 Acc.89-90/029, Vol.37, File 57-G(s); Manifests of SS Radnik - Analysis of Repatriation Movement to Yugoslavia), the number of returnees from the Abitibi region during the years 1947-51 were:
Duparquet (2); Bourlamaque (7); Perron (1); Val d'Or (4); Malartic (9); Normetal (3) / Total: 26
Also see Milovan Mracevich, The Motives of the Croatian-Canadian Pro-Communist Returnees of 1947-48, M.A. (History) University of British Columbia, 1988.
183. LAC, RG26, Volume 144, file 3-41-8 (volume 1), Miners – General File.
184. LAC RG118, acc.1977/78/03, Box 12, file 11-5-3-5-5 pt.3; Employment and Labour Market Industry Studies - Mining
185. LAC, RG146, CSIS File, 27 November, 1946
186. LAC, RG146, CSIS File, 9 May, 1947
187. *The Val D'Or Star*, 26 September, 1947; Ray Price, *Yellowknife*, Peter Martin Associates, Toronto, 1967, p. 297; Geddes Webster, *The Prospector's Pick, The People of the Yellowknife Gold Boom, 1936-1951*, Trafford Publishing, 2007, p. 172. Michael Matthews passed away in Oshawa on 25 August, 1965 (*The Oshawa Times*, 26 August, 1965) and John Matthews passed away in Toronto on 22 July, 1957 (*The Toronto Star*, 22 July, 1956).
188. *The Val D'Or Star*, 30 May, 1965; Marchulenko (1906-1963) passed away in Westmount (Montreal).
189. *The Val D'Or Star*, 11 December, 1953. Frank Gryciuk/Graciuk (1906-1964) passed away in Montreal.
190. LAC, Department of Labour, RG27 Vol. 3021, File: Canadian Metal Mining Association Submission re: Immigrant Labour, July, 1947. In some cases, the mining companies specifically requested miners according to their ethnocultural origin, for example, the Hard Rock Gold Mines in Long Lac asked for Ukrainian miners.
191. For more detailed information on the 'bulk labour schemes' to allow Ukrainian Displaced Persons to settle in Canada, see Myron Momryk,

Ukrainian DP Immigration and Government Policy in Canada, 1946-1952, in Wsevolod W. Isajiw, Yury Boshyk and Roman Senkus (eds.), *The Refugee Experience: Ukrainian Displaced Persons After World War II*, CIUS Press, Edmonton, Alberta, 1992.

192. The price of gold and its effect on the prosperity of a gold-mining community is discussed in *The Gold-Mining Community, A Study of the Problems of Economic Growth,* William Loughheed Associates, Toronto, 1958.

193. For further information on the role of the Canadian Metal Mining Association in recruiting DP miners see: LAC, Department of Labour, RG 27 Vol.279, File 1-26-6 (Vols.1, 2) 1947-56; for information on the experiences of Lithuanian DPs in the Val-d'Or region, see the study by Milda Danys, *DP Lithuanian Immigration to Canada After the Second World War*, Multicultural History Society of Ontario, Toronto, 1986, p.116-117, 123-125,251.

194. *The Star*, 7 November, 1947; John Kostuik (1911-2004) was a graduate of Queen's University and in 1955 was appointed mine manager of Blind River uranium operation, a mining project owned by Steve Roman (*The Star*, 5 August, 1955). His biography is also in the study by George Lonn, *Men and Mines,* Pitt Publishing Company, Toronto, 1962, p.75; see also, *La Gazette du Nord*, 24 October, 1947; Obituary, *Globe and Mail*, 31 December, 2004.

195. *La Gazette du Nord*, 24 October, 1947

196. LAC, RG27, Volume 235, file 1-28-1 (Volume 1), Letter dated 4 June, 1948 from A. MacNamara to Mr. Robert Haddow, Director of Organization and International Representation for Canada, International Fur and Leather Workers Union (Montreal).

197. The problem of the lack of housing in Val-d'Or for Canadian veterans and others is discussed in the autobiographical account by Joan Walker entitled, *Pardon My Parka*, McClelland and Stewart, (Toronto, 1954). The housing shortage was caused by the lack of residential building during the Second World War and the lack of building materials after the war. (See *General Report of the Minister of Mines of the Province of Quebec for the Year Ending March 31$^{st}$,* 1948, p. 37). In Montreal, the shortage of housing for Canadian veterans prompted the CPC to organize 'La ligue des vétérans sans-logis' as a protest movement.

198. LAC, RG27, Volume 3533, file 3-26-38-22, Lamaque Gold Mines Limited, 19 January, 1949. Information obtained in an interview with Mr. Trochym Ryndenko, who arrived as a DP miner and worked two years in the Lamaque Mine before moving to Toronto. He left for Toronto after experiencing two rock-bursts at the mine. Mr. Ryndenko was from Nykolaev in southern central Ukraine and completed technical school in the Soviet Union. He also taught Ukrainian school for a short period

in Val-d'Or prior to leaving for Toronto. He was one of the Displaced Persons who left his wife and family in Ukraine.
199. LAC, RG146, CSIS File, 11 March, 26 March, 1948
200. *Novyi Shliakh*, 21 April, 1949.
201. Zenovy Knysh (ed.), Toward National Unity, *op.cit.*,P.34.
202. See *Propamiatna Knyzhka, Posviachennia i Vidkryttia Ukrainskoho Natsionalnoho Domu,* Toronto, Ontario, 1950; Donors from Val-d'Or were Volodymyr Borsuk, Mykhailo Bzovyn, Ivan Lenyk, sr, Ivan Lenyk, jr., Evhen Khryptak.
203. *Novyi Shliakh,* 8 April, 1950; The teacher was Evdokia Stasiuk.
204. The names of the Ukrainian Catholic clergy were: Rev. N. Chornij (1940-42), Rev. S. Borys (1942-46), Rev. M. Sulatycky (1946-48), Rev. M. Horoshko (1948-49), Rev. S. Shavel (1949-50), Rev. H. Ciupka (1950-51). This information is included in the article by Rev. L. Chayka, *Les Ukrainiens de Val D'Or, Québec,* (8 pages, n.d.) Société d'Histoire de Val D'Or, Val D'Or, Québec.
205. For a short biography, see my article entitled, Father Michael Horoshko, Ukrainian Canadian Army Chaplain - 1944-1946 in *The Archivist,* July-August, 1989. The Father Michael Horoshko fonds is located at the LAC in Ottawa.
206. *Montreal Gazette,* 12 April, 1948
207. *The Globe and Mail,* 25 August, 1947.
208. *The Globe and Mail,* 2 April, 1948.
209. *The Globe and Mail,* 2 May, 3 May, 4 May, 1948; *The Toronto Daily Star,* 3 May, 1948.
210. LAC, RG146, CSIS, 98-A-00185, pt.2, Volume 4945, Special Branch Monthly Bulletin, May-June, 1948, p. 346.
211. LAC, RG146, CSIS File, 12 April, 1948
212. *Narady i Ukhvaly, 2nd National Congress of the Association of United Ukrainian Canadians,* 12-15 January, 1946, Winnipeg, Manitoba (Toronto, 1946) p.15 also; *Narady i Ukhvaly, 3rd National Congress of the Association of United Ukrainian Canadians, 12-15 February, 1948, Toronto,* (Toronto, 1948) p.17, 45.
213. *The Canadian Tribune,* 3 April, 1948; Nazi Stormtroopers Brought to Canada Hired by mine, bush barons; uniformed SS immigrants practice Hitler violence.
214. Criticism of immigrants - work of Reds, Andrew Robertson, manager of Golden Manitou Mines, *The Star,* 11 March, 1949.
215. LAC, RG146, CSIS File, 11 December, 1948; also John Kolasky, *The Shattered Illusion, The History of Ukrainian Pro-Communist Organizations in Canada,* PMA Books, Toronto, 1979, p.103; Kolasky states that '... In Val d'Or, Quebec, they invaded a membership meeting of the AUUC and the police had to be called to eject them ...'

216. LAC, RG146, CSIS File, 23 March, 1949.
217. *The Star*, 15 April, 1947.
218. LAC, RG146, CSIS File, 15 September, 1949
219. House of Commons, *Debates*, 10 March, 1949.
220. Ibid.,
221. LAC, Department of Labour, RG27 Series B2, Acc.73/43, Vol.3533, File 3-26-38-22, Memorandum: Displaced Persons and Mining Employment in the County of Abitibi (18 March, 1949).
222. *The Star*, 7 January, 1949.
223. *Department of Labour, Annual Report for the fiscal year ended March 31, 1955*, (Ottawa, 1955), p. 35.
224. *The Star*, 7 April, 5 May, 1950.
225. LAC, RG2 (18) vol. 249, file I-50-5-M (1948-49). There were also fatalities among the newly arrived miners. For example, Piotr Malowski, age 31, arrived in Canada on 11 February, 1948 and worked at the Consolidated Beattie Mines Ltd. in Duparquet died on 28 June, 1948 in a mine accident. Also, Rudolf Dombrowskis, age 24, came to Canada on 11 February, 1948 and worked at the O'Brien Gold Mines Ltd. in Kewagama, Quebec died on 17 July, 1948 as a result of a mine accident.
226. These incidents are mentioned in the study by Milda Danys, *DP Lithuanian Immigration to Canada After the Second World War*, Multicultural History Society of Ontario, (Toronto, 1986), p.113.
227. *The Star*, 15 July, 26 August, 1949.
228. McKenzie Porter, Val D'Or: Halfboots and High Heels, *Maclean's Magazine*, 1 December, 1949.
229. LAC, MG26 L Volume 135, File P-30-4; Montreal Star, 30 October, 1950; *New York Herald Tribune*, 24 October, 1950.
230. *The Star,* 21 April, 1950; The executive of the UNF Branch were: President- Herman Sawiuk; Vice-President- Michael Harminiuk; Secretary- C. Berezowski; Past President- B. Poremsky, and Dimitri Chalykoff. Evdokia Stasiuk was a teacher in Halychyna and arrived as a Displaced Person to Val D'Or. She then moved to Toronto and became active in the Ukrainian community in Toronto. When she passed away, she donated her estate to the Canadian Institute of Ukrainian Studies (CIUS) in Edmonton. With this endowment in 1988, CIUS established the Stasiuk Program for the Study of Contemporary Ukraine in 1990. (*CIUS Newsletter*, 2014)
231. McKenzie Porter, Val D'Or: Halfboots and High Heels, *Maclean's Magazine*, 1 December, 1949.
232. *General Report of the Minister of Mines of the Province of Quebec for the Year Ending March 31$^{st}$, 1949*, p. 36-37.
233. *La Gazette du Nord*, 13 October, 1949
234. *La Gazette du Nord*, 10 November, 1949

235. T.M.McGrath, *History of Canadian Airports*, Lugus Publications, Supply and Services Canada, 1991, p. 241.
236. *The Star*, 6 April, 1951.
237. William Darcovich (ed.), *A Statistical Compendium on the Ukrainians in Canada, 1891-1976*, University of Ottawa Press, Ottawa, 1980, p. 70.
238. *The Star*, 27 April, 1951.
239. See Appendix: Statistics of Baptisms, Marriages and Death in the Ukrainian Catholic Parish based on information held at La Société d'histoire et de généalogie de Val-d'Or
240. Yarema Gregory Kelebay, *The Ideological and Intellectual Baggage of Three Fragments of Ukrainian Immigrants: A Contribution to the History of Ukrainians in Quebec (1910-1960)*, PhD Concordia University, 1992, p. 207-208, 222.
241. Entry for Ukrainian Youth Association in Volume V, St-Z, and also Nationalism in Volume III, L-Pf, *Encyclopedia of Ukraine*, University of Toronto Press, Toronto, 1993.
242. *The Star* (Val-d'Or) 23 February, 1951; In November, 1951, Peter Wolanek, a World War II veteran, enrolled again in the Canadian Army during the Korean War but died due to unknown causes en route to Val-d'Or while on leave on 12 August, 1952. He was buried in the Roman Catholic cemetery in Val-d'Or in a military ceremony (*The Star*, 29 August, 1952). See also the file on Peter Wolanek in LAC, Personnel Records Centre.
243. Bohdan (Bob) Stasyshyn married Jeannine Lavoie on 18 July, 1954 and this wedding was the first in the newly built Ukrainian Catholic Church. For his contributions to the local community, Bob Stasyshyn (1933-2015) was awarded the Queen's Diamond Jubilee Medal in 2013. For information on Ukrainian Canadians serving in the Korean War, see Myron Momryk, Ukrainian Canadian Soldiers in the Korean War, 1950-1953, *UAV Tribune*, (Ukrainian American Veterans) February, 2014.
244. LAC, RG146, CSIS File, 18 February, 23 September, 2 October, 10 October, 27 October, 16 November, 1950
245. On Sunday evening, 8 October, 1950, a bomb was placed outside the AUUC Hall in Toronto which exploded during a concert and damaged the building. Some AUUC members blamed the recently arrived DPs especially former members of the Halychyna Division for placing this bomb. The Toronto Police launched an investigation of this event but the results were inconclusive. See LAC, RG146, Records of CSIS, Vol. 23, file 93-A-00050, Bombing of Association of Ukrainian Canadians - Ukrainian Labor Temple for the period 50.09.05/50.11.08 and wallet/50.10.08 also LAC, RG146, Vol. 25, file 93-A-00062, Bombing of (8-10-50) Association of United Ukrainian Canadians - Ukrainian Labor Temple - Toronto, Ontario from 9-11-50 to 30-11-50.
246. LAC, RG146, CSIS File, 15 December, 1950, 25 January, 14 February,

1951; events were held in the homes of Andrew Bizyk and Mike Huculiak.
247. LAC, RG146, CSIS File, 8 July, 8 September, 1951; *The Globe and Mail*, June 30, 1951, Anti-Red Squad Grabs Pamphlets in North Raid.
248. *The Globe and Mail*, 8 November, 1951. He was also known as Metro and Mike Karleczak, Karlaschuk.
249. LAC, RG 25 B3, Vol.3175, file: Gold Industry Strike (1953).
250. The differences at the political level between the local branches of UNF and CYM trace their origins to the leadership conflicts that developed in the Ukrainian nationalist movement at the beginning of the Second World War in Halychyna (western Ukraine). The political differences between the two groups of Ukrainian nationalists were also rooted in the competition and conflict between the Melnyk and Bandera factions of the Organization of Ukrainian Nationalists for control of the underground resistance movement in Ukraine during the Second World War. The Bandera faction attempted to dominate the resistance movement to prevent the spread of various independent movements (Atamanschyna) that contributed to the collapse of the struggle for independence during the War of National Liberation in 1918-1921. The nationalist movement during the War and in the DP Camps in Germany became divided between the 'Banderivtsi'(followers of Stepan Bandera) and the 'Melnykivtsi'(followers of Andry Melnyk) that, in Canada, functioned as miniature political parties in most Ukrainian communities. For further information on the historical background of the Ukrainian nationalist movement, see the study by John A. Armstrong, *Ukrainian Nationalism*, (3rd edition), Ukrainian Academic Press, Englewood, Colorado, USA, 1990.
251. Archives of Ontario, Ukrainian Canadian Papers, F1405, Series 56, MU 9232. For a history of the local SUM branch, see Mykhailo Muzychka, Oseredok SUM im. Bohdana Khmelnytskoho - Val d'Or, Kvebek, p.132-136 in Mykola Figol (ed.), *25 Rokiv SUM Kanady, 1948-1973*, Kraiova Uprava SUM v Kanadi, Toronto, 1973. The first members were: M. Muzychka, M. Iavorskyi, I. Mudryi, M. Andrusyshyn, I. Taniuk, P. Zbihlyi, S. Dziamara, S. Zarytskyi, Halyna Sereda, I. Vozniak.
252. List of names of individuals from Val-d'Or and Bourlamaque who sent greetings to the XVI convention of the Ukrainian National Federation held in Winnipeg, 28 June-1July, 1952 and published in the Jubilee Souvenir Book, *Pamiatkova Knyha*: From Val-d'Or- Mykhailo Sorokosky, Julian Berezovsky, Mykhailo Borsuk, Oleksa Hnatiuk, Ivan Kliuchkovsky, Joseph Kliuchkovsky, H. Saviuk, Ivan Saviuk, Volodymyr Salamanchuk, Ivan Svyryd, Ivan Smoly, Mykhailo Stasyshyn, Petro Iuskiv; From Bourlamaque - Vasyl Poremsky, Mykhailo Salamanchuk, Olena Salamanchuk. Herman Saviuk was a member of the Control Commission of the Provincial Executive in Eastern Canada.

253. It should be mentioned that the local Minister of the Jehovah Witnesses was Max Danyleyko, a Canadian of Ukrainian descent who was 25 years old in 1953. However, the focus of their activities was the French Canadian community and there were no recorded contacts with members of the Ukrainian community (*The Star*, 17 July, 1953). Max Danyleyko later became a Jehovah Witness missionary in Haiti.
254. For a short biographical note on Rev. Lev Chayka, see Mykhailo H. Marunchak (ed.), *Biographical Dictionary to the History of Ukrainian Canadians*, Ukrainian Academy of Arts and Sciences in Canada, Winnipeg, 1986, p.668.
255. Multicultural History Society of Ontario, Interview with Reverend Lev Chayka, 10 July, 1979, Val d'Or, Quebec, Interviewer Mary Stefura. Fr. Chayka later claimed that he arrived in Val-d'Or on 1 October, 1952.
256. *L'Echo Abitibien*, 6 September, 2013.
257. For example, among the 13 new members enrolled in the Val d'Or Brownies in 1955 were N. Gaichuk, Mary Kluchkowski, Mary Kostiuk, Carol Lewicki and Natasha Zapototsky (*The Star*, 25 February, 1955).
258. A local census published in *The Star*, 6 August, 1954 indicated that the European population (foreign tongues) had a highest percentage of landlords (rental property):

|  | Census | Landlords |
|---|---|---|
| Total population | 9,466 |  |
| French-speaking | 7,706 | 1,147 (14.8%) |
| English-speaking | 436 | 72 (16.6%) |
| Foreign tongues | 1,324 | 337 (25.4%) |
| Catholics | 8,722 | 1,351 |
| Protestants | 611 | 140 |
| Other Sects | 133 | 65 |
| Squatters | 79 |  |

259. William Warwarniuk (Warwaruk) and Tony Myslowka were on the Protestant School Board in 1947 (*The Star*, 5 September, 1947). William Warwarniuk, a town councillor and school trustee, died at the age of 52 in 1954. He came to Canada in 1926 and lived in Val-d'Or since 1935 (*The Star*, 17 September, 1954). For a brief history of the Protestant school, see John Petrushka, History of Protestant education in Val d'Or, *The Val D'Or Star*, 8 July, 1949.
260. Joe Stasyshyn attended Upper Canada College in Toronto (*The Star*, 6 September, 1947). Ivan Lenyk's children also attended schools in Toronto.
261. *The Star*, 17 June, 1949, Son of Lamaque Chef to Receive M.A. Degree; Frank Belle later had a successful career in the Federal Public Service in Ottawa working in the area of immigrant integration and multiculturalism.

262. *The Star*, 13 July, 1953; John Petruska, attended Bishop's University on scholarship and later worked in the aero-space industry in California becoming a local legend among the European immigrant community.
263. The question of the integration of immigrants into the English Catholic rather than the French Catholic system is discussed in the study by Roberto Perin entitled *Rome in Canada, The Vatican and Canadian Affairs in the Late Victorian Age*, University of Toronto Press, Toronto, 1990, p. 226-228. It seems that a decision was made in Rome that all Catholic immigrants in North America should integrate into the English system since this was the language and culture of the overwhelming majority population. This decision may have played a role in determining the choice of school systems in Val-d'Or at that time.
264. J.S., Our Communities in Northern Quebec (Val d'Or, Malartic, Rouyn, Noranda), *Svitlo* (The Light), January, 1962, p. 44. Mike Andusyshyn was the rare Ukrainian student who attended the French-language high school in Val-d'Or.
265. A brief history of the Ukrainian Catholic Church is included on pages 386-388 in the study, *Histoire de Val-d'Or des origines a 1995*, (1995) published by the Société d'histoire de Val-d'Or.
266. *The Star* (Val d'Or), 2 October, 1953.
267. *The Star* (Val d'Or), 30 October, 1953. The first members of the Parish Council and the Building Committee were: P. Andrusyshyn, N. Tomtsio, Mykola Litwin, Mykhailo Myzuchka, M. Matsko, Osyp Sereda, Fedir Vorona, Stepan Momryk, I. Khmeliavsky, Mykola Kruk, Hryhorii Diachyk, Mykola Kharabaryk.
268. In the publication, *Histoire de Val-d'Or des Origines à 1995*, (Société d'histoire de Val-d'Or), the following names are included under a photograph on page 387 of the building of the church in July, 1954: Katherine Slobodian, Marie Kluczkowsky, John Kluczkowsky, Stephan Momryk, Nicholas Lytwyn, Stephan Tkachyshyn, Mgr. Leo Chayka, Hryhorij Diachyk, John Nastasiak, Paul Koshilka, Mike Mackiw, Dmytro Romanyshyn, Harry Zahoruk, Theodore Worona, John Ferdorynec, John Kuzma, Peter Kordan, John Smoly, Mike Andrusyshyn, Paul Zbihly, Walter Lemyk, John Chmelowsky, Joseph Kluchkowsky, Nicholas Kruk, Philippe Andrusyshyn, John Mynych, Peter Sarachman, Mike Muzychka.
269. *The Star* (Val d'Or), 9 September, 1955.
270. *The Star* (Val d'Or), 14 May, 1954. A short history of the St. Nicholas Russian Orthodox Church is included on pages 388-389 of the study, *Histoire de Val-d'Or des origines à 1995* (1995) published by the Société d'histoire de Val-d'Or.
271. *The Star* (Val d'Or), 10 December, 1954.
272. For short biographies of three miners in this category see the obituaries

of Osyp Sereda, *Homin Ukrainy*, 8 May, 1985; Petro Sarakhman, *Homin Ukrainy*, 30 April, 1985; Mykola Maksymyshyn, *Nasha Meta*, 29 January, 1986.

273. Yves Cote, *L'Evolution et la régression d'une ville minière*, Duparquet, Thesis L.es L., Université Laval, 1972, p.186.

274. In 1954, there were two branches of the Workers Benevolent Association, Branches 88 (Ukrainian) and 191 (Russian). Some of the members of these branches were: P. Kontsevich, Mary Maskevich, R. Bernei, Maksym Mshar, M. Davyskyba, P. Zhuk. *Zvit i Resoliutsii z 18-oi konventsii Robitnychoho Zapomohovoho Tovarystva Kanady, 6,7,8,9 i 10 lypnia 1954 roky*, (Report and Resolutions from the 18$^{th}$ Convention of the Workers' Benevolent Association of Canada, 6,7,8,9 and 10 July, 1954) Winnipeg, Manitoba.

275. LAC, RG146, CSIS File, 4 November, 1953

276. LAC, RG146, CSIS File, 9 November, 1950

277. *The Star*, 7 November, 1956, 20 February, 1957.

278. For example, Mike Charabaruk, 31 years old, suffered a fractured skull in a mine accident and was rushed to Montreal, *The Star*, 13 May, 1955; Harry Holowickyj, 45 years old, was killed in a mine accident at the Lamaque Mine, *The Star*, 9 June, 1956. On 13 March, 1957, *The Star* reported that nine miners were killed in accidents since the New Year. Between 1925 and 1949, 292 miners were killed in the north-west including those in mines in Rouyn Noranda. (Quoted in Nicole Berthiaume, *Rouyn-Noranda*, p. 42.)

279. LAC, RG25 G2 Volume 2228, file: 11747-L-40 (vol.1), CBC (IS) Ukrainian section, Scripts and Correspondence, Vol.1, March 1953-March 30/54, Ukrainian Miners in Rouen-Noranda, Author: Wolod. Shelest, 8 February, 1954.

280. See obituary in *The Star*, 1 April, 1981; Wasyl Poremskyj was a veteran of the Ukrainian National Army and worked at Lamaque Mine from 1937 to 1968. He died at St. Jean Hospital at Macamic on 26 March, 1981 at the age of 87 years and 11 months. He had family in Ukraine. He is buried in the Val-d'Or Catholic cemetery.

281. J.S., Our Communities in Northern Quebec (Val d'Or, Malartic, Rouyn, Noranda), *Svitlo* (The Light), January, 1962, p.43.

282. Archives of Ontario, Ukrainian Canadian Papers, F1405, Series 56, MU 9232.

283. J.S., Our Communities in Northern Quebec (Val d'Or, Malartic, Rouyn, Noranda), *Svitlo* (The Light), January, 1962, p.45.

284. Rev. Chayka received his M.A. from the University of Ottawa in 1972 and then continued to study for his doctorate also part-time.

285. For a short history of the parish, see Julian Beskyd (ed.), *In the Vineyard of Christ, Yearbook of the Eparchy of Toronto*, Toronto, 1964, p.107-114.

286. *The Star*, 5 March, 1958.

287. *The Star*, 13 August, 29 October, 1958.
288. *The Star*, 31 July, 1957.
289. *The Star*, 9 April, 1958. Although Rev. Shevchenko had a Ukrainian surname, he originated from Vladivostok, Siberia.
290. The decline in population was also experienced by other ethnocultural communities. For example, the local Jewish community did not have enough members for a minyan (10 males) and devout individuals had to travel to Kirkland Lake, Rouyn and Montreal to celebrate the high holy holidays (*The Star*, 5 September, 1956).
291. This event was reported in the newspaper, *Ukrainian Life*, 8 December, 1956. It was also reported in the LAC, CSIS report, RG146, Volume 1, Canadian Slav Committee, part 3851, AH/2003-00074, 23 October, 1956. Among those Ukrainian Canadians who left at this time was George Moskal. He was born in Val-d'Or and his family had moved to Toronto in the early 1940s. He left for Ukraine in the early 1950s with his father and studied at the University of Lviv. He returned to Canada in the early 1980s and later was elected President of the Association of United Ukrainian Canadians (AUUC).
292. Some information provided by Sally Smoly: Vera Lisovskaya worked for more than 40 years as a biologist for the Marine Institute of Odessa, Ukraine. Her knowledge of English allowed her to establish the international partnerships of the Institute with a variety of foreign universities and science programs. She passed away on 22 March, 2018 at the age of 79. She was buried in Odessa.
293. Obituary: Richard Lisovsky died on 12 December, 2016 in Odessa. http://www.iobis.org/2016/12/15/richardlisovsky/
294. LAC, CSIS report, RG146, Volume 1, Canadian Slav Committee, part 3851, AH/2003-00074
295. Ibid.
296. LAC, RG146, AUUC CSIS File, 4 February, 1958
297. LAC, CSIS report, RG146, Volume 1, Canadian Slav Committee, part 3851, AH/2003-00074; *The Star*, 17 September, 1992.
298. *The Star*, 16 October, 1957.
299. *The Star*, 16 May, 1956.
300. *The Star*, 27 January, 1956; Tourigny Tips Ukrainians Emulate Fellows in West.
301. See Myron Momryk, *Mike Starr of Oshawa, A Political Biography*, University of Ottawa Press, Ottawa, 2018.
302. *The Val D'Or Star*, 17 February, 1960.
303. Mike Sorokowski owned the A.J. Grocery on 3rd Avenue that was operated by the Kruk family for many years. Mr. Lesiuk owned and operated his own grocery store.

304. *The Star*, 8 February, 1956.
305. *The Star*, 23 May, 1956.
306. *The Star*, 22 May, 1957; The dancers were Diane Koshilka, Jennie Smoly, Nellie Primak, Stefanie Borsuk.
307. *The Star*, 10 February, 1960; The club had twenty one members and met at the Sigma Hotel.
308. *The Star*, 30 October, 1957 and 8 January, 1958.
309. *The Star*, 26 August, 1970; Headline: Nick Hawryluk grows tomatoes. There was an informal contest with Nick Hawryluk [1896-1978] and others to grow tomatoes that reached ripeness despite the short growing season.
310. *The Star*, 15 January, 1958.
311. *The Star*, 12 August, 1959. When this information with Steve Bizyk's photograph in the RCAF, was published in the Val d'Or *Star*, it was brought to the attention of the local RCMP Detachment that his father was an active member of the AUUC with the resulting consequences.
312. *The Star*, 20 November, 1957; Roman Hawryluk joined the RCAF as a photographer. He was educated at the Percival High School and the New York Institute of Photography (*The Star*, 5 March, 1958).
313. *The Star*, 1 June, 1960; Steve Kluczkowski gets Strathcona Medal (with photograph). Steve was Major of the Percival High School Cadet Corps (*The Star*, 17 February, 1960).
314. *L'Echo Abitibien*, 1 March, 1962
315. Obituary of Michael Steranka, The Gazette (Montreal), 11 April, 2013.
316. Molly Hawryluk was related to the Hawryluk family in Val-d'Or.
317. William Darcovich (ed.), *A Statistical Compendium on the Ukrainians in Canada, 1891-1976*, University of Ottawa Press, Ottawa, 1980, p.70; According to the census figures, education among the Ukrainian population in Abitibi County in 1961 was as follows:

|             | Male | Female | Total |
|-------------|------|--------|-------|
| Class None  | 14   | 25     | 39    |
| 1-4 Classes | 33   | 25     | 58    |
| 5-8 Classes | 56   | 27     | 83    |
| H1-2        | 9    | 12     | 21    |
| H3          | 7    | 6      | 13    |
| H4          | 6    | 5      | 11    |
| H5          | 1    | 4      | 5     |
| Some Univ.  | 2    | 2      | 4     |
| Univ.Degree | 1    |        | 1     |

There were 54 males and 40 females attending school at this time.

Total: 329 / Male (183); Female (146)
Source: 1961 Census; (401) Pop 360 - Cross Classes by Origin 14 for Countys, Provs and Canada, Schooling: Abitibi.
318. *The Star,* 9 September, 1959.
319. *The Star,* 19 October, 1961.
320. *The Star,* 1 February, 1962; Marcel Lesyk's parents settled in the Sheptytsky colony and later moved to Amos where they were the only Ukrainian family. Marcel later became Mayor of Amos and a Liberal Party candidate in the Quebec provincial election.
321. *The Star,* 27 September, 1962.
322. *The Star,* 31 January, 24 October, 1963.
323. Obituary: *Homin Ukrainy,* 23 March, 4 April, 2005. Mykhailo Muzychka was born in Ukraine in 1928. During the Second World War, he left for Germany. After the war, he lived in a Displaced Persons Camp in Germany and arrived in Val-d'Or in October, 1950 with his wife and son, Joseph (Joe) Muzychka.
324. *Homin Ukrainy,* 25 March, 1961.
325. *The Star,* 23 April, 1964.
326. *L'Echo Abitibien,* 26 October, 1961
327. *The Star,* 26 October, 1961.
328. See M. Smolii (Smoly), 25 richchia OYK - Val D'Or, Kv., *Woman's World,* November-December, 1963, p. 28.
329. Jaroslawa Wynnycka, (editor) et al., *Outline of History of Ukrainian Catholic Women's League of Canada, Eparchy of Toronto,* New Horizons Group, Basilian Press, Toronto, 1975. p. 179-181.
330. NAC, RG146, CSIS File, 1 June, 1962
331. The announcement was made in *The Val D'Or Star,* 10 October, 1963; 'Val D'Or RCAF Base to Receive Nuclear Arms.' The presence of nuclear weapons in Val-d'Or became a cause for concern among the security officials. There was some concern that the FLQ may make some attempts to raid this base. Also, on 10 May, 1965, three persons from the Polish Embassy in Ottawa were found parked in the parking lot of the civilian/military airport with cameras and a pair of binoculars. Since they had diplomatic immunity they were simply told to leave. Information on the presence of nuclear weapons in Val-d'Or is discussed in the book by John Clearwater entitled, *Canadian Nuclear Weapons, The Untold Story of Canada's Cold War Arsenal,* Dundurn Press, (Toronto, 1998) p. 206-216.
332. T.M. McGrath, *History of Canadian Airports,* Lugus Publications, Supply and Services Canada, 1991, p. 241.
333. Archives of Ontario, Ukrainian Canadian Papers, F1405, Series 56, MU 9232; For a history of the Val-d'Or SUM branch, see Mykola Figol (ed.), *25 Rokiv SUM Kanady, 1948-1973,* Kraiova Uprava Spilky Ukrainskoi Molodi v

Kanadi, Toronto, 1973. The SUM Branch in Rouyn ceased their activities also in 1963.
334. Obituary: *The Toronto Star*, 15 March, 2005.
335. *The Star*, 6 August, 1964. His father, William Fedorko, owned a grocery store in Perron for many years. (*Phone Book, Val D'Or-Bourlamaque*, May, 1962, P.45.)
336. *The Star*, 25 March, 17 June, 1965.
337. Jennie Smoly led a successful career in the medical field in the United States with her husband, Marvin Caruthers of Boulder, Colorado. Jennie Smoly Caruthers passed away in 2006.
338. *The Star*, 8 July, 1965.
339. *The Star*, 11 December, 1974; 'No English films, low turnout'.
340. *Kalendar Svitla*, 1966, Toronto, p. 202.
341. A short biography of Rev. Haymanowych is located in Mykhailo H. Marunchak, *Biographical Dictionary to the History of Ukrainian Canadians*, Ukrainian Academy of Arts and Sciences in Canada, Winnipeg, 1986, p.128-129.
342. *The Star*, 2 February, 1967. Nick Lytwyn was the trustee of the parish.
343. *The Star*, 29 January, 1967.
344. For a history of Bourlamaque, see Benoit-Beaudry Gourd, *La Mine Lamaque et le Village Minier Bourlamaque, Une Historie de Mine*, Collège de l'Abitibi-Témiscamingue, Rouyn, 1983.
345. William Darcovich (ed.), *A Statistical Compendium on the Ukrainians in Canada, 1891-1976*, University of Ottawa Press, Ottawa, 1980,p.70.
346. NAC, RG146, CSIS File, 14 March, 1969
347. *Zhyttia i Slovo*, 17 February, 1969; The donors were: S. Ostapiv, G. Zapototsky, I. Honcharuk, Ihnat Pipsky, F. Moskal, M. Mivap, H. Shostokov, A. Bizyk, F. Bihal, V.Tykhovetsky, A. Shepel, M. Kalynchuk, T. Syrota, F. Kozol, N. Havryliuk, Philip Hredel, I. Misiura, I. Kelman.
348. NAC, RG146, CSIS File, 14 April, 1969
349. NAC, RG146, CSIS File, 14 March, 1969; 20 May, 1970; 19 February, 1971.
350. *The Star*, 24 May, 1972.
351. *The Star*, 30 November, 1967.
352. *The Star*, 6 September, 1978; Manitou Mines to Shut Down.
353. *The Star*, 3 November, 1971, 26 January, 1972.
354. *The Star*, 12 December, 1973.
355. Nicole Berthiaume, *Rouyn-Noranda, Le Développement d'une Agglomération Minière au Coeur de l'Abitibi-Témiscamingue*, Rouyn, 1981, p. 85, 87.
356. T.M.McGrath, *History of Canadian Airports*, Lugus Publications, Supply and Services Canada, 1991, p.241.
357. Nicole Berthiaume, *Rouyn-Noranda*, Rouyn, 1981, p.109.
358. Zenovy Knysh, *Toward National Unity, op.cit.*, p. 47-48.

359. For example, Paul Koshilka died on 4 June, 1975 in Dauphin, Manitoba (*The Star*, 11 June, 1975); Michael Borsuk died in Burlington, Ontario on 26 September, 1977, (*The Star*, 5 October, 1977); Wasil Poremsky (1894-1981) died in Macamic and was buried in the Val-d'Or Roman Catholic Cemetery.
360. *The Star*, 12 April, 1972; The Polish parish priest, Father Edmund Liesnerski passed away in St. Catharines, Ontario (*The Star*, 3 September, 1975).
361. *The Star*, 18 July, 15 August, 29 August, 26 September, 31 October, 12 December, 1973.
362. For an interpretation of the events in the parish, see the publication, *Lest the Trial and the Glory of the Pioneers be Forgotten, The Jubilee Book Commemorating the 85th Anniversary of Ukrainian Settlers in Canada, Province of Quebec*, produced by the Ukrainian Golden Age Club 'Tryzub' of Montreal, The Basilian Press, Toronto, 1979, p. 108-127; also, for a photographic description of the major events in the parish until 1975, see Julian Beskyd (ed.), *Eparchy of Toronto, A Quarter of a Century on the Episcopal Throne, 1948-1972*, Nasha Meta, Toronto, 1975, Ukrainska Katolytska Parokhiia Sviatoi Pokrovy, Valdor, Kvebek, p. 537-543. The editor noted that Rev. Lev Chayka had submitted a manuscript of 140 pages on his work in northern Ontario and Quebec with an addition of 137 photographs but this information could not be included in this publication because it would have required another volume. He suggested that Rev. Chayka publish his own story of the 'Siberian' north in a separate publication.
363. See newspaper article by Alex Radmanovich entitled, Congregation dwindling, but Father Chayka going strong, in the *Winnipeg Free Press*, 8 October, 1975; Priest continues work in Quebec – Despite dwindling number of parishioners, *Svoboda, The Ukrainian Weekly*, 26 December, 1975; Also, see article by Germain Lyrette entitled, Moins d'ukainiens dans notre région, in *L'Echo*, 22 October, 1975. A more optimistic description of the community is included in the article by Michel Brindamour entitled, Les Ukrainiens dans le Nord-Ouest, in the journal, *Education Québec*, Volume 10, no.3. nov-dec 1979.
364. *The Star*, 5 March, 1975
365. *The Star*, 10 November, 1976.
366. *The Star*, 1 December, 1976.
367. Jaroslawa Wynnycka, (editor) et al., *Outline of History of Ukrainian Catholic Women's League of Canada, Eparchy of Toronto*, New Horizons Group, Basilian Press, Toronto, 1975, p. 181.
368. *The Star*, 18 January, 1978, Ukrainians celebrate with Rev. Leo Chayka; 15 November, 1978, Golden Anniversary of the Ukrainian Community in Northwestern Ontario; 6 December, 1978, Ukrainians hold brilliant ceremonies.

369. *The Star*, 2 September, 1981.
370. On 22 December, 1975, 15 people including visitors attended services in the Russian Orthodox Church; *The Star*, 15 January, 1975.
371. *Russkoye Slovo v Kanade*, (Toronto) October, 1980, Article by H. Moiseyev, Four Icon-Lamps.
372. ANQ - Rouyn-Noranda, Fonds de la Société d'Histoire des Anglophones, 08-y, P151/2; *The Star*, 21 April, 1982.
373. According to the 1981 census, the Ukrainian population in Abitibi that was 15 years and over having highest level of schooling was:
Total: 140; Elementary-Secondary: 130; Other Non-Univ.: 5; University with Degree: 5
Source: Census 1981; Abitibi, SDC 81B23 SP24 (Quebec); There were also 135 Poles in Abitibi at this time.
374. For examples, see obituaries of Dmytro Romanyshyn, *The Star*, 27 September, 1972, Nick Lytwyn, *The Star*, 22 August, 1973, Iuri (George) Zapototskyi, *Zhyttia i Slovo*, 3 May, 1982; Mykhailo Havryliuk, *Novyi Shliakh*, 16 September, 1989; There is also an interview with George Zapotoski held on 9 June, 1978 in Val-d'Or; Interview UKR-4052-ZAP, Multicultural History Society of Ontario, Toronto, Ontario.
375. Among those who left Val-d'Or as a result of advanced years and passed away were: Paulina Sikorsky (Toronto and Ottawa), O. Chayka-Havryliuk (Ottawa), M. Liakhovych (Ottawa), Natalie Andrusyshyn (Toronto), M. Sakharnatska (Toronto). Obituary: Natalie Andrusyshyn, *Toronto Star*, 30 July, 1996.
376. *The Star*, 23 January, 1985.
377. See *The Gazette*, Montreal, 16 May, 1987; also Ian Allaby, Val D'Or Enjoys its Role on Road to James Bay, *Canadian Geographic*, (February-March, 1982) p.22-29; Henry Jaworski, Boomtown, *Report on Business Magazine*, March, 1988; Bernard Paré/Chrys Goyens, Val D'Or, Worth its Weight in Gold, *Airmag Via Nordair*, Vol. II, No.5 (1982).
378. Kerry Knoll, Focus on Val D'Or, *The Northern Miner Magazine*, January, 1987, p. 39.
379. T.M. McGrath, *History of Canadian Airports*, Lugus Publications, Supply and Services Canada, 1991, p. 241.
380. Among those members of the AUUC that passed away were Ivan Misiura, Obituary, *Zhyttia i Slovo*, 12 April, 1982 and Yury Zapototsky, Obituary, *Zhyttia i Slovo*, 3 May, 1982.
381. *The Star*, 17 July, 1985.
382. *The Star*, 18 January, 1978. Ukrainians Celebrate with Rev. Leo Chayka.
383. *The Star*, 22 April, 1987.
384. *The Star*, 20 January, 1988.
385. Ibid.,

386. L'Echo Abitibien, 19 juin, 2017 – Une 2e vie pour l'église ukrainienne de Val-d'Or.
387. Novyi Shliakh (New Pathway), 28 November, 2002.
388. John and Mary Smoly moved to Sarnia, Ontario in August, 1992. John Smoly passed away in 1999. Mary Smoly, born in 1921, passed away on 18 February, 2011 in Sarnia.
389. Oksanna (Zbihlyj) Crawley, A Trip Down Memory Lane, *More of Our Canada*, March, 2016.
390. *Federation News and Views* (The Ukrainian Canadian Professional and Business Federation), Second/Third Quarter, 1992, p. 4, Nicholas Tomcio.
391. George Tuhachevsky, from Oshawa; *The New Pathway*, 30 July, 1992.
392. L'Echo Abitibien, 6 septembre, 2013. The journalist made an error when she mentioned that only 10,000 Ukrainians perished during the Famine in Soviet Ukraine in 1932-33.
393. For information on the interpretive centre, see www.campspiritlake.ca http://www.ucc.ca/2016/01/26/marking-the-100th-anniversary-of-spirit-lake-internment-camp-in-2015/
394. For a short history of the colony, see Jaroslav Rozumnyj, One Immigrants Saga: The Sheptycky Colony in Quebec, (The saga of Pylyp Andrusyshyn, 1896-1976) in *New Soil - Old Roots, The Ukrainian Experience in Canada*, edited by Jaroslaw Rozumnyj, Ukrainian Academy of Arts and Sciences in Canada, Winnipeg, 1983; See also newspaper article 'Ambitious Plan for Ukrainian Settlement Failed', *The Oshawa Times*, 1 October, 1975; also by Lily Tasso entitled, Sheptetski: une colonie ukrainienne d'Abitibi aujourd'hui disparue, in *La Presse*, Montreal, 6 July, 1986.
395. Zorianna Hrycenko, Quebec's 'Sheptytsky Colony' Forever Remembered with Ukrainian Flag Raising at La Morandière City Hall, Ukrainian Voice, 10 October, 2016.
396. L'Echo Abitibien, 29 mai, 2018.
397. Denys Chabot et al., Au Coeur des artère de Val-d'Or, Histoire de ses noms de rues, La Société d'histoire et de généalogie de Val-d'Or, 2015, p. 135.
398. Odette Vincent, *Histoire de l'Abitibi-Témiscamingue*, IGRC, 1995. References to the Ukrainian community are found on pages, 330, 383, 395, 530.
399. In the conclusion to his article on the history of the Val-d'Or SUM branch, Mychailo Muzychka wrote that the history of the community in retrospect, Val-d'Or was for the DP generation another 'transit camp' on the way to the larger industrial centers in eastern Canada. (*25 Rokiv SUM Kanady, 1948-1975*, Toronto, 1973, p.135-136)
400. In the 1991 Census, it was reported that the total population of Val-d'Or was 23,840 with French-speaking as 22,050, English-speaking as 865 and non-official languages as 345 persons. The number 345 persons included members of all ethnocultural groups including Ukrainians. (*Statistics Can-*

*ada, Cat. no.95-325, Profiles*, p. 830). It should be noted that these figures were estimates based on the use of short and long census forms.
401. For a discussion on the influence of age cohorts on ethnocultural groups, see the article by Richard D. Alba, Cohorts and the Dynamics of Ethnic Change (p. 211-228) in Matilda White Riley (ed.), *Social Structures and Human Lives,* Sage Publications, Beverly Hills, California, 1988.
402. For the purposes of this study, Canadianization may be considered as an evolutionary process and generational phenomena which is completed when the parents and, in some cases, the grandparents are born in Canada. For most Canadians, their knowledge of their family history does not extend beyond their grandparents. For a local Québécois perspective on the history and integration of the non-French-speaking part of the community, see the article by Nicole Bien, Val-D'Or, Harmony in practice, *Language and Society*, Number 47, Fall, 1994, p. 37-40.

# Bibliography

## Newspapers and Periodicals

*Edinost*
*Kanadiiskyi Farmer (Canadian Farmer)*
*Party Builder*
*Slobodna Misao*
*The Daily Clarion*
*La Gazette du Nord*
*La Presse*
*The Gazette (Montreal)*
*The Globe and Mail*
*The Northern Miner*
*The Oshawa Times*
*The Star (Val d'Or)*
*The Toronto Star*
*The Val D'Or Star*
Maclean's Magazine
*Narodna Hazeta (The People's Gazette)*
*Novyi Shlakh (The New Pathway)*
*Ukrainski Robitnychi Visti (Ukrainian Workers' News)*
*Zhyttia i Slovo (Life and Word)*.

## Archives

- ANQ(Quebec); Lettres patentes de terres, Post-Confederation, Canton: Lamorandière, Cote:M-015.
- Archives of Ontario, Ukrainian National Federation Collection, Val d'Or Branch, Records 1936-37.
- Canadian Museum of History, Archives, The Prokopchak Family fonds.
- Corporation des cimetières de Val-d'Or
- Department of National Defence
- Report of the No. 1 Canadian War Crimes Investigation Unit on Miscellaneous War Crimes Against Members of Canadian Armed Forces in the European Theatre of Operations, 9 September 1939 to 8 May, 1945, Part II.
- Library and Archives Canada (LAC) Ottawa
- Federation of Russian Canadians fonds R151715-O-X-E
- LAC, Department of Labour, RG27

- Orders-in-Council, RG2 Series I, Number 1232, 25 June, 1927.
- Records of the Canadian Security and Intelligence Service (CSIS), AH/2003-00074 - RG146, Volume 1, Canadian Slav Committee, part 3851.
- Records of the Canadian Security and Intelligence Service (CSIS), RG146, File number 93-A-00170, Association of United Ukrainian Canadians, Val d'Or-Bourlamaque, Quebec.
- Records of the Canadian Security and Intelligence Service (CSIS), RG146, Federation of Russian Canadians in Val d'Or, Quebec, Volume 1, part 3861, Request no. AH-2003/00074
- Passenger Lists (1925-1935)
- Tracy Philipps Papers, MG30 E350
- Ukrainian National Youth Federation of Canada Collection, MG28 V8.
- UNYF Historical Research Project, Interview with Ivan Michael Lenyk, 23 June, 1982 (Interview by Taras Pidzamecky).

La Société d'histoire et de généalogie de Val d'Or
P211 Fond Lev Chayka
P255 Myron Momryk
P484 Alex Hnatiuk
P507 John Polenchuk
P657 Donna Kalynchuk


Publications

- Camille Adam (et al.), *Gold in Our Veins, Historic site of the Old Lamaque Mine*, Corporation du Village-Minier-de-Bourlamaque, 2013.
- Aitken, Hugh G.J., *American Capital and Canadian Resources*, Harvard University Press, Cambridge, 1961.
- Berthiaume, Nicole, *Rouyn-Noranda, Le Développement d'une Agglomération Minière au Coeur de l'Abitibi-Témiscamingue*, Collège du Nord-Ouest, Rouyn, 1981.
- Beskyd, Julian (ed.), *In the Vineyard of Christ, Yearbook of the Eparchy of Toronto*, Toronto, 1964.
- Biega, Alexander and Myroslav Diakowsky, *The Ukrainian Experience in Quebec* (1994).
- Bien, Nicole, Val-D'Or, Harmony in practice, *Language and Society*, Number 47, Fall, 1994.
- *Bottin Abitibi-Témiscamingue Directory*, 1935, Rouyn.
- *Canadian Mines From the Air*, Airmaps Limited, Toronto, 1937.
- Chabot, Denys, Jean l'Houmeau et Jean Robitaille, *Perron Pascalis*, Société d'histoire de Val D'Or, 1996.

- Darcovich, William (ed.), *A Statistical Compendium on the Ukrainians in Canada, 1891-1976*, University of Ottawa Press, Ottawa, 1980.
- Duguay, Joseph, L'Abitibi quand on l'habite, Le Bulletin des Agriculteurs, Octobre, 1942.
- *Friends in Need, The WBA Story, A Canadian Epic in Fraternalism*, Winnipeg, Manitoba, 1972.
- Gaudreau, Guy, Sophie Blais, Kevin Auger, *Mine, travail et société à Kirkland Lake*, Collection Agora, Editions Prise de parole, Sudbury, 2016.
- Gauthier, Mme Annette, *Genèse de nos paroisses regionales (Nord Ouest Québécois et est Ontarien)* Rouyn, 1972.
- *General Report of the Minister of Mines of the Province of Quebec for the Year Ending March 31$^{st}$, 1942*, (Quebec, 1942).
- *General Report of the Minister of Mines of the Province of Quebec for the Year Ending March 31$^{st}$*, (Quebec, 1948)
- Gourd, Benoit-Beaudry, *Mines et Syndicats en Abitibi-Témiscamingue, 1910-1950*, M.A. (History), University of Ottawa, 1978.
- Gourd, Benoit-Beaudry, *La Mine Lamaque et le Village Minier Bourlamaque, Une Historie de Mine*, Collège de l'Abitibi-Témiscamingue, Rouyn, 1983.
- Hunchak N.J., *Canadians of Ukrainian Origin, Population*, Winnipeg, 1945.
- Juteau, Danielle, The Sociology of Ethnic Relations in Quebec: History and Discourse, *Lectures and Papers in Ethnicity* No.2, January, 1991, Robert F. Harney Professorship and Program in Ethnic, Immigration and Pluralism Studies, Department of Sociology, University of Toronto.
- Kelebay, Yarema Gregory, *The Ideological and Intellectual Baggage of Three Fragments of Ukrainian Immigrants: A Contribution to the History of Ukrainians in Quebec (1910-1960)*, PhD Concordia University, 1992.
- Keywan, Zonia, *A Turbulent Life: Biography of Josaphat Jean OSBM, 1885-1972*, Clio Editions, Montreal, 1990.
- Keywan, Zonia, *Sheptytsky: A Ukrainian Settlement in Abitibi* (1985)
- http://www.fatherjeanfoundation.org/settlement
- Knysh, Zynovy (ed.), *Toward National Unity, Fifty Years of Service by the Ukrainian National Federation 1932-1982, Historical Almanac*, Volume I, Part 2, Toronto, 1982.
- Kolasky, John, *The Shattered Illusion, The History of Ukrainian Pro-Communist Organizations in Canada*, PMA, Toronto, 1979.
- Krawchuk, Peter, *The Ukrainian Socialist Movement in Canada, 1907-1918*, Progress Books, Toronto, 1979.
- Krawchuk, Peter, *Our Contribution to Victory*, Kobzar, Toronto, 1985.
- Laflamme, Jean, *Les Camps de Détention au Québec durant la Première guerre mondiale*, Montreal, 1973.
- Land, John B., *A Lion in a Den of Daniels – History of the International Union of Mine, Mill and Smelter Workers in Sudbury, Ontario, 1942-1962*.

- Lucas, Rex A., *Minetown, Milltown, Railtown, Life in Canadian Communities of Single Industry*, University of Toronto Press, Toronto, 1971.
- MacDowell, Laurel Sefton, *Remember Kirkland Lake, The Gold Miners' Strike of 1941-42,* University of Toronto Press, Toronto, 1983
- Maceluch, Daniel, How Ukrainians were exiled to Quebec gulag, *The Gazette*, May 11, 1985.
- Marshall, John, *Gold*, Lugus Publications, 1994.
- Martynowych, Orest, *Ukrainians in Canada, The Formative Period, 1891-1924*, Canadian Institute of Ukrainian Studies Press, University of Alberta, Edmonton, 1991.
- Melnycky, Peter, Badly Treated in Every Way: The Internment of Ukrainians in Quebec During the First World War in Alexander Biega and Myroslaw Diakowsky (eds.), *The Ukrainian Experience in Quebec*, The Basilian Press, Toronto, 1994.
- Momryk, Myron, The Royal Canadian Mounted Police and the Surveillance of the Ukrainian Community in Canada, *Journal of Ukrainian Studies*, Volume 28, No. 2, 2003.
- Momryk, Myron, The Ukrainian Community in Val D'Or-Bourlamaque, Quebec, in Alexander Biega and Myroslaw Diakowsky (eds.), *The Ukrainian Experience in Quebec*, The Basilian Press, Toronto, 1994.
- Momryk, Myron, Ukrainian Volunteers from Canada in the International Brigades, Spain, 1936-39: A Profile, *Journal of Ukrainian Studies*, 16, No.1-2, (Summer-Winter 1991).
- Momryk, Myron, Ukrainian DP Immigration and Government Policy in Canada, 1946-1952, in Wsevolod W. Isajiw, Yury Boshyk and Roman Senkus (eds.), *The Refugee Experience: Ukrainian Displaced Persons After World War II*, CIUS Press, Edmonton, Alberta, 1992.
- Moore, E.S., *American Influence in Canadian Mining*, The University of Toronto Press, Toronto, 1941.
- Palmer, Bryan D. and Robin Lunn, The Big Sleep: The Malartic Mine Fire of 1947, *Labour/Le Travail*, 39 (Spring, 1997).
- Porter, McKenzie, Val D'Or: Halfboots and High Heels, *Maclean's Magazine*, 1 December, 1949.
- Prevost, Arthur, *Par La Croix et La Charrue*, Editions Princeps, Montreal, 1939.
- Price, Ray, *Yellowknife*, Peter Martin Associates, Toronto, 1967.
- *Propamiatna Knyzhka, Posviachennia i Vidkryttia Ukrainskoho Natsionalnoho Domu,* (Memorial Book on the Blessing and Opening of the Ukrainian National Home) Toronto, Ontario, 1950.
- Quebec, Department of Mines and Fisheries, *Mining Industry and Statistics, 1937,* (Quebec), 1938.
- Roberts, Leslie, Valley of Gold, *Maclean's Magazine*, December 1, 1934.

- Rozumnyj, Jaroslaw (editor), The saga of Pylyp Andrusyshyn, 1896-1976) in *New Soil - Old Roots, The Ukrainian Experience in Canada*, Ukrainian Academy of Arts and Sciences in Canada, Winnipeg, 1983.
- Smoly, Mary, Viddil OUK u Val d'Or in Irene Knysh (ed.), *In Service of Our Homeland, The Ukrainian Women's Organization of Canada - 25th Anniversary (1930-1955)*, Winnipeg, n.d.
- Stefura, Mary, The Process of Identity: A Historical Look at Ukrainians in the Sudbury Area Community, in *Laurentian University Review*, Vol. XV, No.1, November, 1982.
- Tasso, Lily, Sheptetski: une colonie ukrainienne d'Abitibi aujourd'hui disparue, *La Presse*, Montreal, 6 July, 1986.
- Trepanier, Paul, *Living in Bourlamaque, Memory and Heritage Site of the Bourlamaque Mining Village Historical House*, Corporation du Village-Minier-de-Bourlamaque, 2015.
- *U Pershi Rokovyny 1938-39*, (On the First Anniversary 1938-39) Saskatoon, Saskatchewan, 1939.
- *Val D'Or, 1979*, Chaumont, Anjou, 1979.
- Villemure, Marcien, *Les Villes de la Faille de Cadillac*, Conseil Economique du Nord-Ouest Québécois, Rouyn, 1971.
- Vincent, Odette, *Histoire de l'Abitibi-Témiscamingue*, IGRC, 1995.
- Webster, Geddes, *The Prospector's Pick, The People of the Yellowknife Gold Boom, 1936-1951*, Trafford Publishing, 2007.
- Wynnycka, Jaroslawa (editor) et al., *Outline of History of Ukrainian Catholic Women's League of Canada, Eparchy of Toronto*, New Horizons Group, Basilian Press, Toronto, 1975.

# Index

Abitibi 12, 21, 23, 24, 27, 28, 29, 53, 59, 60, 70, 77, 80, 84, 102, 115, 117, 120, 131
Amos 12, 23, 27, 30, 33, 37, 48, 88, 123
Anglophone(s) 53, 84, 92, 94, 96, 113, 118, 120, 133
Association of Ukrainian Canadians 57
Association of United Ukrainian Canadians (AUUC) 11, 57, 70, 72, 77, 78, 85, 86, 103, 104, 115, 116, 119
Association of United Ukrainian Canadians (AUUC) Women's Branch 72
Bandera, Stefan 85, 87, 99, 104
Borecky, Bishop Isidore 88, 95
Brosko, Peter Paul 62
Cadillac (Town) 53, 73, 84
Cadillac Malartic Mines 32, 73
Canadian Security and Intelligence Service (CSIS) 11
Canadian Slav Committee 12, 70
Canadian Slovak League 39
Canadian Ukrainian Association 64
Caouette, Real 79
Chalkykoff, Dimitri 47
Chateau Inn 57, 59
Chayka, Fr. Lev (Leo) 12, 88, 95, 96, 100, 104, 107, 110, 115, 118, 119, 121, 123, 124
CKVD 66, 89, 100, 101, 113
Cold War 34, 67, 85, 86, 91, 104, 112
Committee to Aid the Fatherland 57
Communist Party of Canada 13, 14, 47, 49, 51, 52-54, 56
Council of Canadian South Slavs 70
Croatian Fraternal Union 70
Czecho-Slovak Anti-Fascist Organization 64
Department of Labour 80, 81
Department of National Defence 83, 117
Department of Transport 117
Depression (1930's) 14, 18, 28, 30, 31, 33, 35, 38, 39, 46, 134
Diefenbaker, Prime Minister John 105
Displaced Person(s) 15, 19, 66, 67, 70, 72-75, 78-80, 82-86, 88, 90, 98, 104, 123, 133, 135
Duparquet 53, 73, 79, 84, 88, 98, 115
Duplessis, Premier Maurice 105
East Malartic Mine 32, 69, 80
Federation of Russian Canadians 12, 56, 57, 63, 64, 66, 67, 70, 79, 85, 102, 112

Fedorkow, Dmytro 62
Finnish Hall 48, 65, 67, 75, 78, 79, 85, 86
Finnish Organization of Canada (FOC) 85
Finnish Workers Club 48
Greek Catholic Church 27
Greek Orthodox Church 12
Gregoraszczuk, Iwan 24
Haymanowych, Rev. Yaroslaw 115
Heron, Rev. Lorne T. 81, 82, 92,
Horoshko, Father Michael 76
Informants (RCMP) 14
International Brigades 46, 48
International Mine Mill and Smelter Workers Union 50, 61, 87
Jean, Father Josaphat 27, 28, 29, 127
Joint Slav Committee 67
Kapuskasing 26
Kirkland Lake 48, 124
Koltak, Watsik 70
Konovalets, Col. Evhen 43
Korean War 85
Koulomozine, Theodore 67, 97
Labor Progressive Party 74, 105
Lac Castagnier 28, 53, 68, 84, 88, 119, 120, 128
Lamaque Mine 32, 33, 37, 38, 42, 45, 53, 61, 73, 75, 117, 120
League of Croatian Canadians 77
Lenyk, Ivan 38, 42, 55, 68
Lithuanian miners 80
Luhovy, Yurij 125, 127
Malartic 12, 32, 33, 48, 49, 50, 53, 55, 56, 57, 66, 69, 73, 79, 84, 88, 115, 117
Malartic Progressive Group 48
Manitou-Barvue Mine (Golden Manitou) 32, 61, 117
Marocco Club 66
Matagami 123
Matthews (Matviiv), John (Jack) 30, 31, 32, 72
Matthews Gold Mines Limited 31
Maxim Gorki Club 48
May Day 77
Moskal, Frank 45
Mshar, Max 85
Muzychka, Mychailo (Michael) 99, 107, 110, 113
Myslowka (Myslanka), Tony 58, 85
National Transcontinental Railway 21, 30

Noranda Mines 31
Organization of Ukrainian Canadian Women (OYK) 44, 112
Organization of Ukrainian Nationalists [OUN] 43, 85, 99
Padlock Law 47, 50, 86
Parti Québécois 118
Pascalis 31
Percival High School 83, 121
Perron 12, 53, 55, 57, 62, 73, 84, 88
Polish Army Veterans 71
Polish Canadian Mutual Aid Society 81, 117
Poremsky (Poremski, Poremskyj), Wasyl 77
Press Fund Committee 71
Prokopchak, Peter 56
Quebec Provincial Police 47, 54, 86
Quebec Referendum (1980) 118
Quebec Referendum (1995) 123
Relief of Russian Refugees Committee 57
Roman Catholic Church 39, 41, 76, 92, 125
Rouyn-Noranda 12, 33, 38, 41, 44, 48, 79, 86, 88, 98, 107, 124
Roy, Oscar 103
Royal Canadian Air Force (RCAF) 83, 85, 110, 112, 115, 117
Royal Canadian Mounted Police (RCMP) 12, 13, 41, 50, 52, 53, 55-60, 64, 65, 67, 86, 98, 104, 112, 115, 116
Russian Orthodox Church 14, 96, 97, 98 102, 119
Russian Relief Fund 57
Serdar, Steve 54
Shavel, Fr. S. 82
Sheptetski (Sheptytsky), Met. Andriy 12
Sheptetski Colony 12, 29, 127, 128
Shevchenko, Father David 102, 119
Sigma Mine 32, 53, 73
Siscoe Gold Mines 30, 32, 37, 53
Siscoe Island 38
Sladen Malartic Mine 32
Spirit Lake 23, 25, 29
Spirit Lake Internment Camp 12, 24, 26, 125, 127
St. Laurent, Louis 82
Stalin, Joseph 60, 70, 102, 103
Starr, Hon. Mike 105
Stasyshyn, Bohdan (Bob) 85
Sullivan Consolidated Mines 32, 37, 78, 117
Terecio, Vasyl 77

Tetrault, Mayor Oza 82
Timmins 86
Tito, Marshal Joseph 64, 70
Tomcio, Nicholas 123
Ukrainian Canadian Association (Ukrainian) School 56, 58, 59
Ukrainian Canadian Association 58, 59
Ukrainian Canadian Civil Liberties Association 125
Ukrainian Canadian Committee 67
Ukrainian Catholic 42, 93, 97
Ukrainian Catholic Brotherhood 100
Ukrainian Catholic Church 12, 88, 89, 106, 112, 114, 118, 122
Ukrainian Catholic Church hall 106, 113
Ukrainian Catholic Women's League 100, 112, 118
Ukrainian Catholic Youth 100
Ukrainian Committee to Aid the Fatherland 55, 56
Ukrainian Communist Youth Federation 54
Ukrainian Labor Farmer Temple Association (ULFTA) 26, 41, 46-52, 54-58, 64, 65, 72
Ukrainian Labor Farmer Temple Association hall 48, 104
Ukrainian National Federation (UNF) 40, 42-44, 52, 54, 55, 60, 61, 64, 67, 68, 75-78, 82, 84, 85, 88, 91, 99, 101, 112, 117, 119
Ukrainian National Federation (UNF) hall 40, 52, 64, 68, 76, 78, 101, 106, 107, 117, 122
Ukrainian National Youth Federation (MUN) 44, 61
Ukrainian Orthodox 93, 97, 101
Ukrainian Orthodox Church 28
Ukrainian School (also Ridna Shkola) 43, 50, 76, 89, 99, 111, 113
Ukrainian War Veterans Association 40
Ukrainian Youth Association (CYM) 85, 87, 88, 89, 90, 91, 95, 99, 113, 136
Ukrainian Youth Club 72
United Steel Workers of America Union 86, 87
Ustutschenkov, Rev. Fedor 102
Val d'Or Historical Society 12
Val d'Or Anti-Communist Committee 77
VE Day (May 8, 1945) 63
Warwaruk, Virginia (Vera) 102
Waskan, Stefan 68
Wiktor, Rev. Father Titus 77
Workers Benevolent Association (WBA) 41, 52, 54, 56, 59, 64, 67, 70, 103, 119
Young Communist League (YCL) 47
Zapototsky, George 79, 85
Zownir, Jerry Roman 38

# NOTES

# NOTES

www.ingramcontent.com/pod-product-compliance
Lightning Source LLC
Chambersburg PA
CBHW070042120526
44589CB00035B/2252